you know you're in
kansas when...

Some Other Books in the Series

You Know You're In Series

you know you're in
kansas when...

101 quintessential places, people, events,
customs, lingo, and eats of the sunflower state

Pam Grout

INSIDERS' GUIDE®

GUILFORD, CONNECTICUT
AN IMPRINT OF THE GLOBE PEQUOT PRESS

INSIDERS' GUIDE®

Copyright © 2006 by Morris Book Publishing, LLC

Text design by Linda R. Loiewski
Illustrations on pages 6, 62, and 81 by Linda R. Loiewski
All other illustrations by Sue Mattero

Library of Congress Cataloging-in-Publication Data
Grout, Pam.
  You know you're in Kansas when— : 101 quintessential places, people, events, customs,
lingo, and eats of the Sunflower State / Pam Grout.— 1st ed.
      p. cm. — (You know you're in series)
  Includes index.
  ISBN 0-7627-3903-7
  1. Kansas—Miscellanea. 2. Kansas—Guidebooks. 3. Kansas—Humor. 4. Kansas—
Description and travel—Miscellanea. I. Title. II. Series.
  F681.6.G765 2005
  978.1'033—dc22

                                                                              2005025932

Manufactured in the United States of America
First Edition/First Printing

This book is dedicated to the children of Iraq and to the hope that someday we adults will be smart enough to lay down our arms and just play.

about the author

Pam Grout is a mother, a playwright, an activist, and a collector of quotes and quirky information. *You Know You're in Kansas When* . . . is her twelfth book. For more information
about Pam's books, her second career as a speaker, and her outside-the-box view of reality,
check out her sometimes-updated Web site at www.pamgrout.com.

to the reader:
there's no place like home

Trying to limit Kansas to 101 quintessential things is like trying to transport the entire Brady Bunch in a Volkswagen Beetle. Can't be done. You could blindfold me, tie my hands behind my back, and make me dance while I'm doing it, and I could still come up with 101 historical events, 101 places, 101 customs, and certainly 101 interesting dishes. How many states make wheat nubs, for instance?

But my illustrious editors at Globe Pequot, who have to worry about such petty details as the cost of paper and ink, were forced to rein me in, to insist that I do my very best to whittle down the list of Kansas fascinations to a mere 101. And I tried, I really did.

I had to cut out, "You know you're in Kansas when you've seen people wear bib overalls to funerals and weddings." And I had to leave out major details about the dozens of grassroots artists who make Kansas such a remarkable place. I didn't mention Herman Divers, the retired hospital handyman who made a full-size Harley-Davidson out of 179,200 pop can pull tabs, even once. Wouldn't have been fair to Steve Gray, who made one out of 10,000 bones, or Inez Marshall, who carved one out of a giant slab of post rock limestone. And the tourist attractions I had to omit . . . well, the Kansas Travel and Tourism Department will probably demand my head.

In short, I can only apologize to everyone who didn't get mentioned. Greg, Marcia, and Alice, I'm sorry I couldn't squeeze you into the VW Bug. If it makes you feel any better, I did think about you. *Obsess* might be a better word. I lost sleep over which 101 quintessential "things" to include.

Not to rationalize, but limits have always been a problem for me. In sixth-grade art class, when all the other kids did stencils with one color of paint, I opted for a whole kitchen scene with a potbelly stove, a Christmas tree, presents, and eight different colors of paint. I figured a holiday scene deserved nothing less.

And neither does the state of Kansas. It's by far one of the most interesting of the 50, yet it has never, like Rodney Dangerfield, gotten the respect it deserves. If people had any idea, they'd be flocking here in droves. We might even have to pave some of the roads to our tourist attractions.

I tried tracking down the source of all the ugly rumors, the ones that insinuate that Kansas is drab, flat, and boring. But like the person who outed Valerie Plame, the CIA spy, I fear getting to the bottom may well be beyond my reach.

I do believe I've narrowed it down to two, maybe three suspects.

The first, out-of-state motorists on Interstate 70, can't really be blamed. They're trying to get to grandma's house in time for her 86th birthday. Or out to the ski slopes before the snow melts. It's a shame they can't see beyond those green-and-white interstate signs announcing the vast miles to St. Louis or Denver, but that's just human nature.

Our boys in Topeka, now, they didn't start the rumors, either. They've seen the sunsets, tasted the rain, experienced the spring watercolors wash over the Flint Hills. They know good and well how glorious our state is. They just don't see the point in hitting other people over the head with it. I mean, nobody knew who Kelly Clarkson was, either . . . until she won *American Idol*.

Which brings up the last suspect for the genesis of the rumor: the mass media. Specifically, *Life* magazine. On September 21, 1959, the iconic magazine published an article contrasting the values of middle-class Americans living in Hutchinson, Kansas, and bohemians known as "beatniks" from Venice, California. The article, titled "Squaresville, U.S.A. vs. Beatsville," showed the clean-cut citizens of Hutchinson gazing at family photo albums, visiting grain elevators, and swimming in the local pool. Sure, we do all those things in Kansas, but so do people in California, Florida, and New York. Follow-up letters to the editor of *Life* had the nerve to suggest that Kansas was "enervatingly dull" and "inherently mediocre." My hunch is they've never been here.

I guess the *Life* article just proves two things. One, the media is extremely powerful. And two, they don't always get things right.

In the case of Kansas, *Life* was way off. Kansas, to those of us who've taken the time to look, is stunning. Its landscape, its skies, its rich history could never in a million years pass for either dull or mediocre. Except to an idiot who jumped to conclusions.

For a while, I was one of those idiots. I couldn't wait to get out of "Squaresville, U.S.A." to see the parts of the world that all the big travel magazines touted. I lived in a ski town, joined a commune, met people from all over the planet. Like I said, limits are not my thing.

But what I came to realize, what finally drew me back, is something a famous Kansan once said: "There's no place—and I do mean NO place—like Kansas."

you know you're in
kansas when...
...lunch can be had for a buck

It's probably true that there's no such thing as a free lunch. But at Frannie's Lunchroom in Yates Center, you can get mighty close. Lunch at Frannie's costs 10 thin dimes. Monday through Friday. Drinks included.

Frannie's is about as unpretentious as you can get. The daily special, hand-scrawled on a piece of notebook paper, is tacked to a wall. None of the dishes, cups, tables, or chairs match. But when you climb the 31 steps to reach the restaurant where Frannie herself greets each customer personally, you feel as if you just stepped into Grandma's house. Don't even think about getting out the door without introducing yourself.

Frannie—whose real name is Francis Ward—started the joint 20 some years ago after her husband had a stroke. Medical bills started mounting, so Frannie, who had raised three kids and never worked outside the home, started cooking for the county jail. Somebody suggested that she open a restaurant.

After she found the perfect space—the third floor of Light Hardware, a 100-year-old building on the downtown square—and paid the $150 rent, she was flat broke. "I had to borrow $5.00 from my nine-year-old granddaughter," she says.

$1.00

The price of a home-cooked meal in Yates Center. There's only one entree every day, but it comes with salad, a vegetable, and your choice of coffee, tea, or Kool-Aid.

Frannie's
Daily Special
Meatloaf.....$1.00
comes with salad,
a vegetable, and
your choice of
coffee, tea,
or Kool-aid

When you finish a meal, Frannie trusts you to pay the bill. She leaves the cash register open by the front door. Just stick your dollar in or make change if you need to. Unless, of course, you want pie. Then you must leave $2.00. "The cash register is electric," says Frannie, "but I've never bothered to plug it in."

kansas when...

...everything's only 30 minutes away

Ask Kansans where the next town or the closest open gas station is, and they'll answer, "Oh, about 30 minutes that-a-way," or point you "roughly 30 minutes due south." It's a joke of sorts, but according to Beverly Hurley, public relations officer for the Travel and Tourism Division of the Kansas Department of Commerce, it's not too far from true.

"I've driven all over this state, taken my kids practically everywhere, and it's usually about 30 minutes from one town to the next," she says.

Plug in "30 minutes away in Kansas" into Google, and you'll get more than a million hits, many on Web sites such as the town of Westmoreland's, which states the following sales pitch: "Westmoreland is less than 30 minutes from any other point in the county."

That's how we describe things around here. But in between the towns that admittedly might be an exercise in anal-retentive land

30 minutes:

The time it takes to get from point A to point B in Kansas.

planning are the real measures of Kansas— the land, the sky, and a horizon that may not be endless, but sure seems that way.

When the Symbols of Agriculture public awareness project kicked off in 1978, each Kansas farmer was feeding only 56 folks (55 people + you). Or at least that's what the big grocery bag said on the 8- by 8-foot signs that dot major Kansas highways.

By 1999, the last year the statistic was published by the U.S. Department of Agriculture, each Kansas farmer was feeding 129 people (128 + you). That's a big responsibility, not only for the farmers with all those mouths to feed, but also for the Kansas Agri-Women, who started the sign project to promote state agriculture. About the time they'd get "55 + you" or "82 + you" up on the sign, the USDA would come out with a revised figure, and somebody would have to climb up again and apply a new decal.

When the USDA stopped computing the figure (saying that the demands of the changing agriculture industry made it too difficult), the Kansas Agri-Women breathed a sigh of relief and figured they'd just leave the climbing toll at 128 + you.

It sure as heck eliminated a lot of confusion. "We'd send those decals out to local members who lived near the signs," said Jeanne Mertz, a longtime board member, "but some folks wouldn't get the decals up as fast as others. So we'd get a call asking how come one signs says 98 and another says 102?"

128 + You:

The number of people a farmer feeds, according to a familiar roadside sign seen only in Kansas.

Besides, maintaining a network of 60 outdoor signs (the grocery bag sign had cousins promoting wheat and beef) was a lot of work for a small organization, especially when many of the members were in their 70s.

Themeatrix.com, a takeoff on the popular movie starring Keanu Reeves, features Moopheus, a cow in a trench coat on a clandestine mission. In the clip, Moopheus tells an innocent pig named Leo about the real story of industrial agriculture and factory farming.

The cleverly produced, award-winning clip doesn't exactly say whether Leo's peaceful, idyllic farm is in Kansas, but the message certainly applies. Like everywhere else, small family farms in Kansas are being swallowed up by giant corporations. Only a fourth of the remaining farms in this country are family operations, and only 6 percent of all farmers are under the age of 35.

Given these trends, many farmers have been forced to fight back with what's known in the industry as agritourism. In other words, farmers and ranchers must open their land to the public. One of the most popular draws, at least in Kansas, has been corn mazes, which can bring as many as 50,000 paying customers to the farm. At $7.00 a pop, that's a mighty fine supplement to the yearly wheat income.

The Martisko and Gaeddert farms near Buhler, for example, have used their fields and 10-foot-tall stalks of corn to create mazes shaped like giant palm trees and dolphins, the Statue of Liberty, a lighthouse, and

Noah's ark. They also have a pumpkin patch, hayrack rides, and a country store that sells farm-grown produce and craft items. Over the last six years, these farmers have gotten so good at designing mazes that they are now also able to supplement their incomes with corn-maze consulting.

Agritourism:

1. Farm- or ranch-based tourist attractions. 2. An alternative form of income for small farms and ranches.

Although it has been referred to from time to time as the Nile of the Midwest, the country's fourth largest river is known by most people in this country as the Arkansas. As in "R-kin-SAW," with accents on the first and last syllables, like the state from which Bill Clinton hails. But in Kansas, this 1,450-mile river is known as the "r-KAN-sas." Don't even think about mentioning that other, inferior pronunciation.

We admit that this discrepancy causes a few tongue-twistings, as was the case when a high school band from Arkansas City (a town of about 19,000 on the Arkansas River) marched in the Rose Bowl Parade. The emcee made the mistake of announcing that our proud purple-and-gold bulldogs were from that other state, the one with the mongrel hogs (I believe they call them razorbacks). It took us a while, but we finally forgave that announcer.

For 26 years in the 19th century, the majestic Arkansas—which, as far as we're concerned, is named after our state—served as the boundary between the United States and Mexico. And it helped wagon trains

Arkansas River:

A wide prairie river that happens to also flow through a few minor neighboring states.

navigate the Santa Fe Trail. Although its headwaters rise up in the Colorado Rockies near Leadville and it eventually meanders into Oklahoma and Arkansas, the "r-KAN-sas," as we proudly say it, runs lengthwise through much of southern Kansas.

you know you're in
kansas when...
... you stumble into the world's smallest presidential library

Unlike most states, Kansas has two presidential libraries. The Eisenhower Museum and Library in Abilene is pretty well known. It's one of 10 presidential libraries administered by the National Archives and Records Administration, and it welcomes thousands of tourists each year.

The other one honors our 12th president—no, not Zachary Taylor (he was the 13th and was born in Virginia). Housed inside the restored Santa Fe depot that serves as the Atchison Historical Museum, the presidential library is little more than a kiosk. Only a few people see it each year.

I should probably explain. David Rice Atchison served as U.S. president for one short day. Which could account for why he's usually left off the official list of former presidents. By a quirk of fate, the proslavery Democrat assumed office when newly elected Zachary Taylor, a religious man, refused to do so on the appointed day. Turns out that incumbent James Polk's term ended on March 4, 1849—the Sabbath. Taylor refused to defile it for something as insignificant as a little oath of office.

As president pro tem of the Senate, Atchison was next in line for the job. During his 24 hours in office, he didn't declare war or appoint any of his cronies to office, but he did turn his unofficial presidency into a great story. The Atchison Historical

Museum has taken its namesake's lead, turning the "world's smallest presidential library" into a great story as well.

The kiosk contains a picture of Atchison, who was born in Frogville, Kentucky; a Civil War pistol he once owned; the one biography written about him; and a copy of his Senate speeches.

Atchison, David Rice:

This unknown former president of the United States claimed that his one-day administration was "the honestest . . . this country ever had."

6

you know you're in
kansas when...

...your neighbors on both sides build airplanes

When millionaire adventurer Steve Fossett decided to fly around the world without stopping or refueling in March 2005, he couldn't have picked a better place than Kansas from which to launch his record-setting flight.

Although his *Global Flyer* wasn't built in Kansas, more than 250 million other aircraft have been built here since 1919. And all of the aviation pioneers—from the Wright brothers to Amelia Earhart to Bill Lear—have ties to Kansas.

Orville and Wilbur Wright, of course, launched the world's first successful flight from Kitty Hawk, North Carolina, in 1903. But their mentor, Octave Chanute, an engineer born in Paris, built the railroad in Kansas and lent his name to the town of Chanute. His 1894 book, *Progress in Flying Machines,* inspired a correspondence with the Wright brothers, who claimed that his research and continual encouragement paved the way for their success. Chanute was even on hand to take photos of their first flight.

Within a few years of that historic event, Kansas was home to 60 airplane manufacturers, including more than a few that never got off the ground. The first commercial air plane, the Laird Swallow, was created in Wichita in 1920. This city in southwest Kansas soon became a hub for such avia-

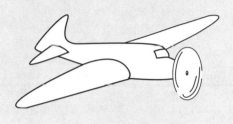

Aviation Industry:

One in nine people in Wichita works in this business.

tion leaders as Glen Stearman, Walter and Olive Beech, and Clyde Cessna, who not only set up shop in a vacant auto factory but also established one of the country's first flight schools.

No wonder inventing genius Bill Lear left Switzerland to launch the first business jet in Wichita. His Learjet factory, next to the Mid-Continent Airport, built 146 craft between 1962 and 1967, when Lear sold it to the Gates Rubber Company.

Known today as the Air Capital of the World, Wichita produces 40 percent of all airplanes built in the United States. It has the world's largest aviation maintenance facility, and between Cessna, Raytheon, Boeing, and Bombardier Learjet, the city sells more than $3.2 billion worth of aircraft each year.

7

you know you're in
kansas when...
...there's an official tour of barns

Well, *official* might be stretching it. The historic barn tour of Doniphan County doesn't have a tour guide or an air-conditioned bus. For that matter, it doesn't even have a bus without air-conditioning. But a brochure is available at the chamber of commerce (located in the bank) in Troy.

This two-color brochure lists several barns that can be driven by, gawked at, and photographed—including the three-story Godfrey Nuzum barn, which is built into a bluff; the Kiehnoff barn, which has a unique system of louvers for getting air in, yet keeping rain and birds out; and the John Fuhrken barn, an octagonal structure that was touted as the "wave of the future" in the late 1800s by the Department of Agriculture.

Indeed, back in the days when Doniphan barns were built, farmers often put more money into their barns than their homes. Although barns are still celebrated as an icon of rural life (the Smithsonian hosted a two-year, eight-state touring exhibit called Barn Again), they are being razed along with the 3.8 million farms that have bitten the dust in the last century.

Barn Tours:

Along with Ghost Town Tours and the Fred Baker House (where Lincoln stayed before giving his famous Cooper Union Address), the hottest ticket in Doniphan County.

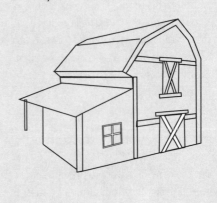

But the iconic wood and stone structures will never lose their place in American consciousness or in the drive-by tour in Doniphan County.

... nobody notices the winter cold because they're too consumed with basketball

A reporter from *Sports Illustrated* once said, "Almost everything that matters in the sport of basketball is somehow connected to Kansas." Kansas, after all, is the state where James Naismith and Phog Allen coached, where Clyde Lovellette and Wilt Chamberlain played, and where Adolph Rupp and Dean Smith learned their trade.

Basketball in Kansas is such a big deal that the Basketball Hall of Fame in Springfield, Massachusetts, is named for Kansas University's first coach (Naismith). It includes more inductees from Kansas than from any other state.

Although there are many great basketball rivalries across the country, few match the statewide interest, crazy gags, and institutional pride of the Sunflower Showdown. So named in 1902, it pits archrivals Silo Tech (as Kansas State University is called by Kansas University) against Snob Hill (as KU is called by K-State).

Students have been known to camp out for tickets in subzero weather, waiting literally days for the chance at an unreserved seat. They also have thrown hot dogs, bananas, and more than just a few insults at whichever team they despise.

And while the origin of the "wave"—the global phenomenon where fans stand and raise their arms in succession—has been credited to everyone from Mexican soccer fans during the 1986 World Cup to the Oakland A's in 1981, Kansas fans know that they've been "waving the wheat," as they call their version of the tradition, for at least 30 years.

> **Basketball:**
>
> 1. A game played on a court by two opposing teams of five players. 2. A Kansas obsession.

you know you're in
kansas when...
...police stop traffic for a Bible parade

If you happen to drive through Humboldt, Kansas, on the first Saturday in October, don't blame me if the police pull you over and kindly ask you to wait. You see, the only things allowed on the town square at 11:00 A.M. on that particular day are floats, the high school band, and other miscellaneous entries in the Biblesta parade. According to the local chamber of commerce, the Humboldt Biblesta is the largest parade in the world depicting scenes from the Bible. Of course, it's possible that it's the *only* parade in the world depicting scenes from the Bible.

Nonetheless, every float, every character, and every entry is bound by tradition to honor the Good Book. The Humboldt High School band leads the parade with the gospel classic "Just a Closer Walk with Thee," and from there you're apt to see everything from Jesus carrying a cross to Jesus getting baptized to the Four Horsemen of the Apocalypse.

The crowd favorite, a 40-foot whale (of Jonah fame) that squirts water on spectators, has retired from official competition, but it has been in the parade every year but two since Biblesta began in 1957.

So if you're in Humboldt the first Saturday in October, just park your car; roll down your windows (at least until the whale goes by, at which time you may want to protect your leather seats); and stick around for great gospel, contemporary Christian music (last year the Zambian Vocal Choir came all the way from Africa), and a free evening bean feed.

Biblesta:

The world's largest parade featuring scenes from the Bible.

kansas when...

... your ancestors started the Civil War

If politicians had stuck to the Missouri Compromise of 1820, which clearly stated that slavery was prohibited above the 36' 30" latitude, Kansas could have entered the Union peacefully, saved itself a lot of bloodshed, and had just one government instead of two.

But politicians, being what they are, turned Kansas into a political football when they revoked that agreement with the Kansas-Nebraska Act of 1854.

Suddenly the newfangled Kansas territory was up for grabs, turning it into a powder keg that would eventually ignite the Civil War. People from both sides of the hotly contested slavery issue poured into the territory, hoping to sway the vote on whether Kansas would be a slave state or a free state.

Secret Dark Lantern societies aimed to intimidate Free Staters, who set up strongholds across the state and armed themselves with Sharps rifles. People on both sides were tarred and feathered, lynched, kidnapped, and killed. There was also rampant election fraud, at least four different drafts of a state constitution, and two rival governments, each outlawing the other. The U.S. Army, outnumbered and often outgunned, was able to do very little.

Bleeding Kansas:

A term coined by Horace Greeley of the *New York Tribune* to describe the violent hostilities between pro- and antislavery forces in the Kansas territory between 1856 and 1861.

In one of the most notorious events, fiery abolitionist John Brown led a group of men in an attack at Pottawatomie Creek. The group, including four of Brown's sons, dragged five proslavery men from their homes and hacked them to pieces with artillery swords.

Violence over Kansas even erupted in the U.S. Congress. After the abolitionist senator Charles Sumner delivered a fiery speech called "The Crime Against Kansas," a proslavery congressman beat him senseless with a cane.

you know you're in
kansas when...
...buffalo still roam

Although virtually all of the 70 million buffalo that once roamed America's prairies are gone forever, Kansas, which pegged the buffalo as its state animal, is as good a place to see them as anywhere. Both Maxwell Wildlife Refuge, a 2,250-acre preserve north of Canton, and Finney Game Refuge in Garden City offer up-close and personal prairie tours of these once-ubiquitous creatures that weigh up to 2,000 pounds, grow up to 6 feet tall, and run fast enough to squash your average jackrabbit.

Ranchers all over the state raise them, and quite a few Kansas restaurants serve up buffalo burgers. Of course, buffalo comes in any cut a cow does, and it's a heck of a lot more nutritious. Bison meat has less fat and fewer calories than beef, pork, chicken, and even sockeye salmon. And besides, whoever heard of Mad Buffalo disease?

The late Ray O. Smith, a Kansas rancher who built a 61-ton concrete buffalo on his property near Longford, used to say, "I'll tell you how smart the white man is. He killed off all the animals that could live easily out here and replaced them with cows that need to be fed three times a day."

Buffalo:

A big, shaggy brown animal that used to exist in herds as big as the state of Rhode Island. The real name is bison, but "Oh give me a home where the bison-o roam" just doesn't have the right ring to it.

you know you're in
kansas when...
...the top tourist attraction is a retail outlet

Arizona's number-one tourist attraction is the Grand Canyon. California's, of course, is Disneyland. In Kansas the top tourist attraction is a four-acre retail store that sells guns, tents, and fishing equipment.

Cabela's happens to have weekly fly-tying demos and workshops on everything from camouflage clothing to how to perform a convincing turkey call. This megastore also has a large collection of life-size trophy mule deer, a walk-through aquarium, an indoor shooting range, a two-story waterfall, and free parking. Last time I checked, Disneyland's parking rang in at $12 per car, and you can't get a car within spitting distance of the Grand Canyon for less than $20.

Cabela's, which has stores in 12 states, was started somewhat inadvertently in 1961 when salesman Dick Cabela came home from a trip to Chicago with more fishing flies than he knew what to do with. From his kitchen table in Chappell, Nebraska, Cabela wrote a classified ad to run in the Casper, Wyoming, newspaper: "12 hand-tied flies for $1." He got all of one response.

Cabela's:

A really, really big store that draws four million visitors to Kansas every year.

Undaunted, he rewrote the ad: "Free introductory offer! Five hand-tied flies . . . 25 cents postage and handling." Before he knew it, Cabela, who was savvy enough to include a mimeographed catalog of other outdoor products with each order, had to recruit his wife and brother just to keep up. Today the company produces more than 76 catalogs each year and has 19 retail outlets, including the one in Kansas, which opened in 2002.

you know you're in
kansas when...
...graveyards are why tourists visit

The 11 life-size Carrara Italian marble statues of John and Sarah Davis in the middle of Mount Hope Cemetery in Hiawatha attract 30,000 visitors a year. Davis, an eccentric farmer who lived frugally until his wife died, sent waist, height, hip, and shoe measurements to Italian sculptors so that the statues of him and his wife at various stages in their life together would be realistic in every way.

Other cemetery tourists have included Kurt Cobain, who made a pilgrimage to the tiny Stull Hill graveyard before his death in 1994. Known as one of the Seven Gates to Hell, this run-down, barely noticeable cemetery has inspired some pretty amazing rumors. Some say the devil's child is buried there. I've also heard that a boy-cum-werewolf haunts the place. The lead singer of Nirvana went to test the most notorious legend: If you throw a bottle against one of the rock walls, it won't break. Or, if it does, you're next to join the dead.

There's also the suitcase gravestone in Lincoln (its honoree, J. S. Jacobs, was a traveling salesman); the backward gravestone in Maple Hill (relatives of Sarah Ann Oliver figured they'd save money on her concrete gravestone by pouring it themselves); the 1924 Chevy motor block gravestone in Garden City (Mitch Runnel's family took what

was left of the 16-year-old's beloved car after it was hit at a rail crossing, affixed it to a slab, and gave it a coat of silver paint); and one of the few glass-enclosed coffins in the world, in Lucas.

Cemeteries:

1. Where people bury the dead.
2. Where people in Kansas get wildly creative.

14

A sign outside the Edwards County Histori-cal Museum in Kinsley reads MIDWAY USA—1561 MILES FROM SAN FRANCISCO AND 1561 MILES FROM NEW YORK CITY.

But even more important to surveyors and mapmakers is a cross mark on Meade's Ranch, 6 miles southeast of Osbourne, that's known as the official geodetic center of the United States. To mapmakers, it's the Greenwich of North America. Every calcula-tion of latitude or longitude anywhere from Mexico to Canada uses this "primary sta-tion," as it's called by the Army Corps of Engineers, as the starting point. Anytime a surveyor checks property lines, he's posi-tioning that property in relationship to Meade's Ranch.

The geodetic center is not to be confused with the geographic center, which is 42 miles north in Smith County. To determine the latter, in 1918 the United States Coast and Geodetic Survey took a piece of card-board, cut out the shape of the lower 48 states, and balanced it on a pin point. The center of the United States (39.25' 50" north longitude and 98.25' 35" latitude, to be exact) just happened to fall in the mid-dle of a hog farm near Lebanon. The locally run Hub Club, thinking that this designation might bring in tourist dollars, installed a pyramidal stone monument with a brass plaque on a hilltop just outside of town.

Center of Everything:

1. The choicest or most essential part of some idea or experience. 2. A point equidistant from either coast. 3. Kansas.

The plaque, which identified the spot as THE GEOGRAPHIC CENTER OF THE UNITED STATES, wasn't exactly correct. The farm was three-quarters of a mile away, but owner Johnny Grib wasn't too keen on turning his beloved property into a tourist trap. Especially when the state government got involved, ponying up the money for a hotel and road crews to pave a 1-mile strip leading to the site.

Unfortunately, the great hordes of tourists never arrived and the hotel was sold to Texas investors who visit only once a year, during hunting season.

you know you're in
kansas when...
...it takes a world treaty to get locals to sit up and notice

Cheyenne Bottoms, the largest marsh in the interior United States, is considered the most important site for bird migration in all of North America, if not the entire western hemisphere. But it wasn't until a 1998 treaty proclaimed the 60-square-mile depression near Great Bend "a wetlands of international importance" that most Kansans realized just what they had.

Nearly half of the North American shorebird population stops over at Cheyenne Bottoms during their annual spring migration. More than 320 different species have been recorded, including many endangered and threatened birds such as the whooping crane, peregrine falcon, least tern, and piping plover.

Even though many Kansans weren't up to snuff on their avian treasure, the Native Americans before them sure were. In fact, Cheyenne warriors, for whom the bottoms are named, fought many battles to keep the natural land sink as their tribal hunting grounds. A battle in 1825 was so fierce that one of the streams running into the bottoms was said to have turned red with blood, hence the name Blood Creek.

Cheyenne Bottoms:

A 41,000-acre network of shallow lakes and marshes located 6 miles northeast of Great Bend.

The Kansas Department of Wildlife and Parks oversees part of this refuge, which includes diverse aquatic habitats—mudflats, pools, and canals, both shallow and deep, salty and fresh, weedy and open. In the 1990s the Nature Conservancy started acquiring and protecting even more of the unique basin.

you know you're in
kansas when...

...people spend time rating chicken-fried steak restaurants

If you got the spring 2003 issue of the *Kansas Explorers* newsletter, you already have your list of Kansas restaurants with the best chicken-fried steak (CFS). The short list, ready to clip out and stick in your wallet, includes 35 restaurants that met the rigorous criteria for the state meal: (1) It has to be hand-breaded. (2) It must be pan- or grill-fried (deep-fat-fried imposters would never make the list). (3) The round steak or cube steak must be fresh, not frozen. It doesn't need mentioning that bonus points are given for homemade gravy and real mashed potatoes.

Restaurants that make the list get an official certificate, many of which are framed and hung somewhere near the kitchen.

The long list, two whole pages, requires folding and even includes days, hours, and tips for getting there first. Pinky's Bar & Grill in Courtland, for example, tends to run out of CFS by 12:30 P.M. Go early.

The only things our lists don't include are calorie counts and fat grams. Why concern ourselves with insignificant details?

There's another breed of CFS lovers who don't carry the list at all. These Kansans prefer to rate their chicken-fried steak restaurants by the number of pickup trucks parked out front. Rule of thumb: Never stop

Chicken-Fried Steak:

1. A steak pounded thin, breaded, fried in hot oil, and smothered in white cream gravy. Usually accompanied by mashed potatoes; the less contrast between meat and vegetable, the better. 2. The state dish of Kansas.

at a one- or two-pickup joint, as the steak will have been frozen and factory-breaded.

Although Texans sometimes like to claim the CFS as their own invention, we happen to know that the very first printed recipe appeared in a Topeka cookbook in 1949.

you know you're in
kansas when...
...going to "the city" requires a list

The city is where you go to have a cavity filled, buy new windshield wiper blades, find the latest *New York Times* bestseller, and stock up on powdered sugar and Metamucil. If there's time left over, you might even take in a first-run movie. You don't go until your list—which usually has two sections (to-do and to-buy) and hangs on the refrigerator with magnets—contains at least three items.

If you live in central Kansas, your city is probably Salina, population 45,679. It's where you go if you live in, say, Brookville, to have a nice meal . . . especially since your only restaurant, the famous Brookville Hotel, picked up and moved to Abilene a few years back. If you're in Liberal, which people in Santanta might consider their city, your city is probably Amarillo, Texas, three and a half hours away. It's where you go when your list contains items like fairtrade, organic-grown coffee or the latest art film.

Depending on where you live and what's on your list, your city could have a population of anywhere from 67,000 (Garden City) to 346,000 (Wichita). If you live in northeast

The City:

Where you do all that needs doing, usually in one trip. Also known as civilization.

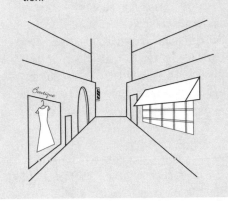

Kansas, your city, even though it bears your state's name, might actually be divided between two states. A road cleverly called State Line Road divides Kansas City, Kansas, from Kansas City, Missouri (those name thieves).

kansas when...

...a covered dish dinner is the best meal in town

Like most places, Kansas has its share of McDonald's and Burger Kings. And, yes, its natives have fallen for the billion-dollar marketing schemes that allow international chains to wipe out local joints. But the best food in Kansas can still be had any weekend at local covered dish dinners.

Churches host covered dish dinners. Women's clubs host them. Schools and civic organizations host them. Heck, in Windom (population 136), which calls itself the Covered Dish Capital of the World, even the volunteer fire department hosts one the first Saturday in December. It's at 6:00 P.M., in case you're hungry.

Walt Whitman, who contributed two poems to the very first issue of *Kansas* magazine and claimed to be a huge fan of our state, couldn't wait to visit as long as he was "not asked to speak nor eat any public dinners." The rest of us know that public dinners, also called potlucks or covered dish dinners, provide the yummiest, most original entrees around.

The competition is informal and nobody would admit it, but Kansans see covered dish dinners as an opportunity to display—and, dare I say, show off—our culinary skills. At such gatherings you're apt to get anything from buffalo sausage to half a dozen versions of the latest recipe in

Ladies' Home Journal to *vareniki* and shoo fly pie, both European Mennonite dishes.

No one has been able to isolate how the covered dish dinner actually started (rarely are the dishes covered), but I'd place my money on the Russian Mennonites who immigrated to central Kansas in the mid-1800s.

Covered Dish:

1. A hot meal baked in a 9- by 13-inch dish, often including hamburger, noodles, and cream of mushroom soup. 2. The main attraction of Kansas dinners held at churches, town halls, and parks.

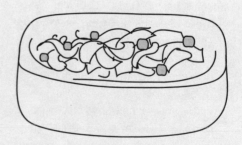

Why waste all that money on plastic chips and bingo cards when you've already got more cows than you know what to do with, plenty of livestock arenas, and folks who are willing to fork over good money to see which square a cow patty lands in?

Yes, in Kansas people play bingo with cows. And the chips? Well, let's just say they're certainly not plastic and they make good fertilizer.

Technically, I guess you could call cow bingo gambling, a pastime frowned on by the legislature in Kansas, but the Atchison Historical Society prefers to call it a fundraiser.

Every year at the Atchison County Fair, right before the livestock auction, the museum divides the livestock arena into a board of 360 squares. People with money (as well as those who can't resist) buy said squares. Then an unwitting steer, whose identity is carefully guarded until the 6:00 P.M. starting time (wouldn't want anyone to have an unfair advantage), is released into the arena. The steer wanders around, waiting to do his business, while crowds in the arena cheer him on, bribe him, and coerce him with food. As loud as it gets, you'd think it was the Super Bowl.

> **Cow Bingo:**
>
> Profitable fundraiser in Atchison, not to be confused with cow Frisbee, another popular Kansas pastime.

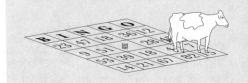

I suppose it all started with Larry Woydziak, a Lawrence fireman who decided to bowl with Martha in every county of Kansas. In case you didn't read "Larry's Gutter Life," the Web journal in which Woydziak detailed his heroic journey, Martha is the mother-of-pearl bowling ball he bought for $1.95 at a local thrift store. It came with a pair of nearly clean socks and a booklet of 1988 bowling coupons.

Woydziak came up with his unusual quest one day at a Kansas Explorers conference. The Kansas Explorers are a wild and wacky bunch of folks who promote local travel and small-town culture. At last count there were 1,800 members, all of whom had forked over $18.61 (the year Kansas became a state) to join. Larry became such a celebrity (huge crowds gathered at the local bowling alleys where he and Martha bowled) that other Kansas Explorers decided to get in on the action. One Explorer decided to eat biscuits and gravy in every county. Another established the goal of jogging through every county.

"Burger Bill" Bunyan, a Dodge City Explorer, downed a hamburger in all 105 counties. It took him three years, but on his 65th birthday (August 21, 2003), wearing a "Living Large" T-shirt, Bunyan ate his 105th burger at Paddy's in Sterling. Fifty of his closest friends were there as witnesses.

Last I heard, there are Explorers out in Kansas buying fabric in every county, spending $18.61 in the smallest grocery store in every county, and singing karaoke in every county. Such efforts may earn one of them the LuWonderer Award, a 10-inch limestone fence post that is secretly passed from member to member to recognize exploring achievements.

Dare to Do Dirt:

Motto of the venerable Kansas Explorers Club, a fun-loving outfit that's always looking for new ways to show state pride.

21

Kansas doesn't have many celebrities (although Willie Aames from *Eight is Enough* used to live in Olathe), so we've had to earn our 15 minutes of fame in more creative ways. Namely, by getting all the major news publications to ridicule our board of education's ongoing debate about evolution.

Back in 1999 the Kansas Board of Education rejected evolution as a valid scientific principle. In a 6-to-4 vote, the 10-member board, ignoring pleas by educators and established scientists, eliminated evolution from the curriculum and deleted it from state testing standards. To say it caused a national uproar is an understatement. The American Civil Liberties Union, which has been involved in the issue since the Scopes monkey trial, threatened legal action. News outlets from the *Washington Post* to ABC News claimed that the decision set Kansas back at least a century, and Linda Holloway, who was chairman of the board, got so many insult-laden messages from around the country that her husband feared for her life.

In the next election several of the "anti-evolution" board members were voted out, and the controversial scientific theory was put back into the state curriculum. But then George W. Bush and his No Child Left

Darwin, Charles:

Originator of the theory that keeps Kansas educators in an uproar.

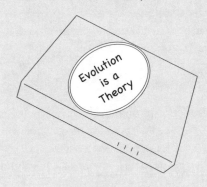

Behind Act brought academic testing back to the table, and Kansas jumped into the evolution vs. creationism fray again. The current attorney general has suggested that textbooks bear a sticker warning students that evolution is not an established fact.

As the issue ping-pongs back and forth, it continues to be a great publicity coup for the confused state of Kansas.

...June means Dorothy training

In Liberal there are 21 Dorothys, all of whom have taken an extensive, two-week course on how to be a tour guide at one of the town's biggest attractions: Dorothy's House and the Land of Oz. All of these rigorously trained Dorothys, ranging from junior high to junior college girls, have either made their own costumes (complete with blue-and-white gingham dress and red ruby slippers) or talked their moms or grandmas into making them. And they're all well versed in the Dorothy rules: no cussing in costume (even the word *butt* is verboten), cell phones must be turned off, and don't even think about asking your boyfriend to show up at work.

Wannabe Dorothys used to apply for the plum positions, but now candidates must be recommended by teachers or church leaders. In junior high being a Dorothy is considered community service, but at age 14 you get paid to lead tourists on first-person tours through your home.

During the busy summer season, two Dorothys are on staff in the morning and two more in the afternoon. A three-year-old girl got upset when her Dorothy, a proper brunette, was replaced at break by a redheaded Dorothy. Thinking quickly, the redhead told the toddler not to worry, she was just Dorothy's cousin.

Perks of the job include getting your photo in books and films. A Canadian filmmaker who produced the documentary *Being Dorothy* for public television filmed one of the clones playing "Somewhere Over the Rainbow" on her harp in the middle of Highway 54. A Japanese film crew brought their own Dorothy, but a Liberal Dorothy got the honor of giving her Japanese counterpart a private tour.

Dorothy:

1. A fictional character who rides a tornado to Oz. 2. A plum position for girls in Liberal, akin to being chosen as homecoming queen.

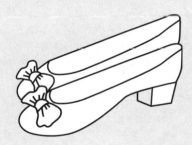

you know you're in
kansas when...
...dust is nearly as haunting as the bogeyman

The Dust Bowl of the 1930s, immortalized by John Steinbeck in his 1939 novel *The Grapes of Wrath,* is long forgotten by most Americans. But in Kansas, where we live with dust, swallow it, and watch it form dust devils, it's a vein in our consciousness that runs thick and deep.

As *Emporia Gazette* columnist Cheryl Unruh said, "We've cleaned dark dust clumps from the corners of our eyes. Some windy days when we wash our hair, the water turns brown from the catch of the day. We're familiar with the race between a pickup and the swell of dust that chases it. The truck arrives at the stop sign first but the dust sails victoriously through the intersection."

The Dust Bowl that lasted from 1933 until 1940 rendered much of western Kansas uninhabitable, as ceaseless winds carried swirling clouds of dust—dust so thick you couldn't see 5 inches in front of your face. Tons of topsoil from every square mile were lifted and carried as far east as New York City. Dust darkened skies for days. It drifted like snow.

By the mid-1930s hundreds of thousands of farmers were forced to abandon their land, fleeing to California and the Sunbelt states. Although high-powered pumps can now reach deep into the Ogalala Aquifer, ensuring that our farmers are no longer dependent on the vicissitudes of weather, there's not a Kansan among us who hasn't seen a dust devil and wondered, "What if?"

Dust:

It's what's for dinner.

... your great-great-grandmother lived next door to Amelia Earhart

No one who knew Amelia Earhart in Atchison, where she was born on July 24, 1897, and lived for the first 10 years of her life, was surprised that she became one of the world's most celebrated aviators and a stellar role model for women everywhere. A well-known tomboy, Amelia attended a private college-prep school along with her sister, Muriel, near their grandparents' Atchison home.

Not only did Amelia have a .22-gauge rifle (she figured she could eliminate bubonic plague if she shot all the rats in her grandfather's barn), she also loved bicycles, basketball, sledding, and adventures of any kind.

Once, she and her sister built a roller coaster track from the top of a tool shed, 8 feet from the ground. After greasing the rickety wooden track with lard, Amelia made the trial run in an empty wooden crate. Going much faster than they had anticipated, Amelia flew off the tracks, tore her dress, bruised her lip, and declared excitedly, "Oh, Pidge [her sister's nickname], it's just like flying."

Fly she eventually did, setting many speed and distance records, including being the first person (not just woman) to make solo flights over both the Atlantic and Pacific Oceans. As she said, "I learned to fly before I learned to drive."

A celebrity, Amelia developed her own fashion line, became friends with Eleanor Roosevelt (who had just gotten a student flying permit when her appointed teacher's plane went down in the Pacific), and married wealthy publisher George P. Putnam, who published her many books. Fan mail let her know that babies, lakes, and even homing pigeons were being named after her.

Amelia and her newly rebuilt Electra disappeared in the Pacific Ocean on July 2, 1937, while she was attempting to make the first around-the-world flight. The U.S. Navy sent 40,000 people, 10 ships, and 65 airplanes and spent $4 million to search for her, unsuccessfully.

Earhart, Amelia:

This famed aviator held many world records—including the most extensive search-and-rescue mission.

you know you're in
kansas when...
...20 years go a long way

Given the way Hollywood has immortalized the Wild West, you'd think the cattle drives from Texas to Kansas lasted for centuries. People from foreign countries have asked me if the saloons in the Kansas cow towns—Dodge City, Abilene, and Ellsworth, to name a few—are still pouring whiskey. And they actually wonder if the notorious sheriffs—Wyatt Earp, Wild Bill Hickock, and Bat Masterson—are still playing poker, flirting with dance hall girls, and chasing outlaws.

For some there was little distinction between *law* and *outlaw*. One year after becoming marshal of Caldwell, Henry Newton Brown used the Winchester rifle the city gave him to rob the bank in Medicine Lodge. Turned out he was a former member of Billy the Kid's gang.

In truth, the cowboy era that so dramatically captured the world's imagination lasted less than two decades. Wild longhorns from Texas (as many as five million) were rounded up and driven to the new railheads in Kansas from about 1866 to the mid-1880s. And most of the rugged cowboys—the heroes who represent that fierce independence we so look for in the mirror—were kids barely wet behind the ears, ranging in age from 15 to 25. Few others were fool enough to make the rugged journey that was known to involve light-

> ### Earp, Wyatt:
>
> Along with his cronies, this notable cow town sheriff has furnished an abundance of material for dime novels, nickelodeons, Hollywood films, radio, and television.

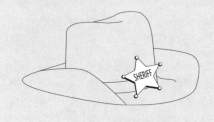

ning, cacti, rattlesnakes, cattle stampedes, tornadoes, and/or floods. Or to accept the salary: $25 to $40 per month.

But because sleeping on a bedroll under the stars and mixing it up with Indians, cavalry soldiers, dance hall girls, buffalo hunters, and other rowdies is such a powerful and persistent image, the Kansas frontier, along with its outlaws, cowboys, and deputy sheriffs, lives on some 130 years later.

you know you're in
kansas when...
...grapes aren't necessarily a vintner's first choice

It's not that Kansans don't use grapes to make wine. There are at least half a dozen wineries across the state that grow everything from French hybrid grapes and German varietals to local Kansas grapes. It's just that the most famous Kansas winery—the one that's won more than 130 national and international awards—makes its wine out of elderberries. And cherries and apples and rhubarb and blueberries and peaches.

Every now and then, Wyldewood Cellars Winery, a family-owned business near Wichita, does make a bottle or two out of grapes, but it has developed a reputation as the largest producer of elderberry wine in the nation. And it's hard to find a town in Kansas that doesn't have a least one liquor store that carries the unique product

It was Margaret Brewer, a nurse, who originally planted her family's 1,000-acre ranch with elderberries Son John, who made wine as a hobby, decided to experiment with his mom's crop. Eight years and 200 formulas later, he took the results to his friend Mike Martini, a famous Napa Valley winemaker, who couldn't taste the difference between wine made with elderberries and that made with grapes.

Could be that the joke's on all those traditional vintners. Not only do elderberries have nine times the vitamin C and seven and a half times the vitamin A of grapes, they're also known to boost the immune system and treat colds, asthma, constipation, colic, hemorrhoids, insomnia, and even sunburn. John and his sister, Merry Brewer, opened Wyldewood Cellars in 1994; they haven't had a cold since. Hippocrates, who prescribed elderberries back in the fifth century B.C., would be pleased. In fact, the Romans used to say that anyone who grew elderberries would die of old age rather than illness.

Elderberry Wine:

Wyldewood Cellars makes this award-winning concoction, which was served at the 2002 Winter Olympics in Utah.

you know you're in
kansas when...
...people equate elevation with breakfast foods

A team of geographers from Texas and Arizona made national headlines when they scientifically "proved" that Kansas is flatter than a pancake. Using topographic data, microscopes, and a perfectly fried flapjack from the International House of Pancakes, the diligent researchers discovered that a pancake—or at least the one they purchased from IHOP—is not as flat as it seems.

In fact, according to Mark Fonstad, lead researcher on the study that appeared in the May/June 2003 issue of the humorous *Annals of Improbable Research,* "If an ant walked on a pancake, it would look like the Grand Canyon."

But the research had problems. As the scientists noted in the article, "Barring the acquisition of either a Kansas-sized pancake or a pancake-sized Kansas, we had to rely on mathematical techniques for a proper comparison."

Using a $500,000 confocal laser microscope at Arizona State University, the three-man team mapped the terrain of a flapjack by cutting it in half, taking a picture of its outline, and scanning it into a computer. Then they compared the data to Kansas elevation data from the U.S. Geological Survey.

Lee Allison, director of the Kansas Geological Survey, was not impressed. "My guess is

Elevation Impairment:

Next to tornadoes and Toto, what Kansas is best, albeit mistakenly, known for.

you could put Colorado in there, the way they're calculating it, and it would be flatter than a pancake. It's part of a vast breakfast food conspiracy to denigrate Kansas." The main problem with their findings, he claimed, is that they included the entire pancake, not just the top part.

According to Allison, Kansas is not even close to being the flattest state in the nation. If you measure flatness as the difference between the highest and lowest elevations, 21 other states are flatter. As Gary Classen, chairman of Liberal's International Pancake Race Day noted, the research did prove one definitive fact: "There are obviously people with way too much free time."

you know you're in
kansas when...
...zoos are run by everyday Joes

Although Kansas has 10 accredited zoos, more per capita than any other state, and offers the country's only four-year degree in zookeeping, it also has a lot of mom-and-pop zoos. For example, the Safari Zoological Park in Caney, with more than 70 exotic animals, is run by Tom Harvey, his dad and mom, and his girlfriend, Rhonda.

"People think since we're out in Kansas that we probably have a couple chickens, a cow and maybe some frogs," Harvey says. Boy, are they in for a surprise. The Caney zoo, which started as a private collection but opened to the public in 1994, has black African bear cubs, white tigers, black leopards, jaguars, and a rare white Barbary lion. People come from China, Australia, and other faraway countries to see the rare menagerie. Harvey, who often gives tours himself, has been known to hypnotize alligators and ride the backs of lions.

The Hedricks Exotic Animal Farm in Nickerson has more than 2,800 animals that Joe Hedricks, a former rodeo clown and bullfighter, rents out to petting zoos and Christmas parades. (His fallow deer make excellent reindeer.)

Originally Hedricks offered camel and pony rides and promoted races between his ostriches, camels, and pigs. Finally, in 1992, he opened the Exotic Animal Farm to the public, adding concession facilities and a bed-and-breakfast that must be the most unusual in the world. Unlike Embassy Suites, where you look out from your room into a courtyard of plants and fountains, the view from Hendricks's B&B windows is into a courtyard filled with kangaroos and wallabies.

Everyday Joes:

The owners of many zoos in Kansas.

you know you're in
kansas when...
... even foreheads have a farmer's tan

Men in Chicago wear Cubs caps. Bostonians prefer ball caps with the Red Sox logo. In Kansas men wear ball caps that promote Dekalb, Asgrow, and other seed brands— unless the people in question are ranchers (there's a big difference between a rancher and a farmer), in which case they sport a cowboy hat. Most likely a Stetson.

But all the foreheads of the men in Kansas—at least the ones who work the land—have one thing in common: a distinct horizontal line dividing the top half of the forehead from the bottom. The upper section is Casper white, having been hidden from sun since Little League. The bottom section has a rich, deep tan, something any Coppertone model would gladly trade her bikini top for.

Not just anyone is likely to witness this strange phenomenon. You pretty much have to be intimate with the aforementioned foreheads, and even that is no guarantee. Some farmers' wives are lucky if their husbands take off their caps to shower.

> ### Farmer's Tan:
>
> Characteristic two-toned coloring of the foreheads of Kansas men who work the land.

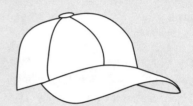

kansas when...

... you have an Abraham Lincoln costume in the back of your closet

I realize that Kentucky is the state that normally springs to mind when people think of Abraham Lincoln. But Kansas lays claim to at least part of the glory. Lincoln's famous Cooper Union address, the speech that propelled his bid for the presidency, was first given in the Sunflower State. And it was 11-year-old Grace Bedell (who moved to Kansas from New York) who suggested to the presidential candidate that with his skinny frame, he ought to consider a beard.

Ever-gracious Abe wrote the young girl a letter thanking her for the fashion advice, and sure enough, by the time he was inaugurated, he was sporting a full beard, the first American president to do so. Despite offers as high as $5,000, the adult Bedell refused to part with her treasured letter, which she stored in a vault in the bank her husband ran in Delphos. Finally, after her death, a television producer bought the famous note for $20,000.

The residents of Lincoln, one of 32 towns in the United States named after our 16th president, have a unique connection as well. A childhood friend of Abe's moved to Kansas and helped settle the town, and as many as 20 of Abe's third and fourth cousins still live in the county. During Presidents' Week they get out their fake beards, dark coats, and stovepipe hats for an Abra-

February 12:

When half the population of Kansas celebrates Abraham Lincoln's birthday by dressing up to look just like him.

ham Lincoln look-alike competition. Unfortunately, only one Abe gets the honor of leading the freedom march.

In addition to this contest, which takes place at high noon on the steps of the historic 1899 limestone county courthouse, there's a passionate recital of the Gettysburg Address, a march led by the local drum and fife corps, and a buffalo luncheon. The latter used to cost one picture of Abe ($5.00), but alas, the price had to be raised. The meal includes buffalo stew, biscuits, apple butter, and a "Lincoln log"—a chocolate-and-cream cake rolled up like a hearth log, of course.

As my dad used to say when driving by oil wells with their distinct, unmistakable odor, "Take it in, kids. That's the smell of money."

In southwest Kansas the smell of money wafts from monster feed lots that can "finish," as they call it, as many as 150,000 cattle at a time. The country's first commercial feed lot was established in Garden City in 1951; today there are more than 60 such operations within a 60-mile radius. Feed lots are basically a bunch of pens with feeding troughs where calves and yearlings are fattened up before being shipped off to slaughter. Only in southwest Kansas, they don't have to be shipped far. Meat-packing plants are just as prolific, if not odiferous, as feed lots.

So what if the smell is not something perfumeries are stampeding to duplicate. It's profitable and it's part of a long-standing tradition in Kansas. Since the 19th century, when most of the major cattle trails ended up in Dodge City, Kansas has been a major player in the growing, transporting, and processing of beef.

Feedlot:

1. A plot of fenced ground on which livestock are fattened for market.
2. Moo-sic to many Kansans' ears.

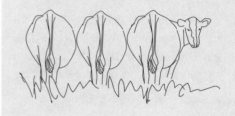

you know you're in
kansas when...

...you can water-ski in the public swimming pool

The swimming pool at Finnup Park, a 110-acre park in Garden City, is big. Put enough adjectives in front of it, and it's the world's largest. But rather than convince you that it's the largest free concrete outdoor municipal pool in the entire known universe, I'd rather tell you that it's big enough to accommodate a motor boat pulling two water-skiers. The city proved that one year in a promotional stunt, as you can see in a photo postcard that's still available at the nearby history museum.

Here are the facts: The swimming pool holds 2.5 million gallons of water, takes up half a city block, and requires 17 lifeguards when the whole thing is open. The Big Dipper, as the pool was known in 1922 when it was first built, was dug completely by hand by volunteers and horses pulling scrapers. Although construction was halted temporarily to get the wheat harvest in, the pool was finished by the enthusiastic community in a few short months.

The Jaycees once hosted bathtub races in it. And elephants from the Lee Richardson Zoo (right across the street) used to take a dip in the pool's water. Thankfully, today it's just the summer splashing ground of many Garden City families.

Finnup Park Swimming Pool:

A football-field-size swimming pool that measures 330 by 220 feet.

you know you're in
kansas when...
...people set fires on purpose

Come spring, ranchers in the Flint Hills get a bunch of kerosene, spread it over their pastures, and start big, blazing fires. On purpose. Not only does this annual prairie burn get rid of dead, nutritionless grass, it supposedly adds an additional 25 pounds of market weight to each steer (the grass that grows back is more nutritious).

This important ritual is quite a sight to behold. Chase County alone has been known to burn more than 400,000 acres of pasture; one year it took only three days.

Before cattlemen began torching their pastures, the Kanza and Osage Indians fired dead grass to lure buffalo, deer, and elk. And before that, Mother Nature did it with lightning.

Environmentalists claim that such clearing is vital to maintaining the rare prairie ecosystem, which once covered 140 million acres in this country. Only 2 percent of the country's native tallgrass prairie remains, most of it in Kansas.

Sometimes the resulting smoke gets blamed for unfit ozone standards in Kansas City, a good 90 miles away. The Kansas Department of Health and Environment wrote a letter to Flint Hills fire chiefs one year, pleading with them to spread the annual burn over several months and to limit themselves to 160 acres at a time.

> **Fire:**
> A necessary thing on the Kansas prairie, where spring blazes clear the way for new growth.

The ranchers, who know good and well that Kansas City's cars and industry cause most of its air pollution, got together over coffee and figured that it would take seven years to burn Chase County if they did it that way.

But they can assure Kansas City's Environmental Protection Agency reps of this: Prairie-burning techniques are quite sophisticated these days, involving lots of people, carefully prepared fireguards, fire trucks, weather monitoring, and even GPS systems.

you know you're in
kansas when...
...the ground beneath you wobbles

You know the phrase *rolling over in your grave?* Well, that's what early Kansas settlers are doing . . . at least those keeping up with current affairs. The rabble-rousers who first settled Kansas would be aghast if they knew how conservative their visionary state has become.

In its early days Kansas was a place of daring social experimentation. Whole communities were established on such progressive concepts as racial equality, vegetarianism, socialism, and open marriage. Hundreds of reform newspapers were published in Kansas, including *Lucifer the Light-Bringer,* a Valley Falls weekly vehement in its quest for equal marriage rights, and the *Appeal to Reason,* a socialist newspaper that in the early 1900s had the largest circulation in the entire country, more popular than either the *New York Times* or the *Los Angeles Times.*

Progressive ideas like eight-hour workdays and the abolition of child labor were hatched in Kansas. The world's first protest march was organized here when 6,000 women, many the wives of coal miners, took to the streets in 1921 to protest the miserable pay and abominable working conditions their husbands were forced to endure.

Kansas once led the way in social, religious, and political freedoms for the entire nation. As William Allen White said, "Things start in Kansas that finish in history."

Unfortunately, that was *so* yesterday. In fact, Thomas Frank, a former Kansan and contributing editor to *Harper's,* wrote a best-selling book on how a former hotbed of leftist activism turned into a solidly red state. In *What's the Matter with Kansas?,* Frank uses Kansas as the classic example of how conservatism, once a marker of class privilege, became the creed of millions of ordinary Americans.

Flip-Flop:

Once famous for its radicalism, Kansas now serves as the buckle of the Bible Belt.

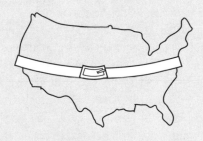

you know you're in
kansas when...
..."state forestry department" sounds like an oxymoron

Just because Kansas is situated on the prairie doesn't mean we don't like trees. Heck, we've got more than 120 varieties on our list of champion trees, which includes 23 different kinds of oaks and a Tree of Heaven that's 69 feet tall and has leaves that smell like rancid peanut butter.

We also have some rather unusual forests, including an official state forest in Pottawatomie County that only has one tree (the Vieux Elm, which ranks as the largest elm tree in the whole country, according to the National Registry of Big Trees). There's also the International Forest of Friendship, which has trees from all 50 states and more than 40 countries, including a cherry tree from George Washington's Mount Vernon estate and a redbud from President Eisenhower's home.

Granted, only 4 percent of our state is forested, and according to a report in a recent issue of *Kansas Canopy* (the newsletter of the Kansas Forest Service), nearly 50 percent of our hardwood trees are unusable for wood products. Nonetheless, the KFS does one bang-up job managing the 2.2 million acres of forests that we do have. The state agency not only maintains the list of champion trees, but also

Forests:

A pleasant surprise on the Kansas prairies.

sponsors a poster competition on Arbor Day, administers the Tree City USA program, and makes sure that we Kansans known how critical trees are to our well-being.

...65-million-year-old fossils are considered art supplies

One day back in 1964, Viola Fick looked down at the ground on her ranch near Monument Rock and saw a lot of fossilized shark teeth (72, to be exact). She and her husband, Earnest, borrowed what Vi called "a learner's book on fossils" from Earnie's nephew, a bona fide college student, and began to search in earnest. Before all was said and done, the amateur paleontologists had found thousands of Cretaceous fossils, including 11,000 fossilized shark teeth, all within a 50-mile radius of Oakley.

After a while the teeth all started to look the same, so Vi did what any sensible person would do: She turned them into art. She made eagles, American flags, the presidential seal, the state seal of Kansas, and, of course, a bas-relief sculpture of a shark—all out of fossilized teeth. One of the eagles had a snake in its talons, but Vi used rattlesnake rattlers for that. She embedded the best teeth in fancy frames that she made to show off her portraits of flowers, trees, and people, all made with melted wax, papier-mâché, paint, glue, and fossils.

In all, Vi made hundreds of artworks from fossilized shark teeth, vertebrae, fish jaws, shells, and crinoids. As one of the curators at the Fick Fossil Museum in Oakley says, "They didn't have cable back then."

Fossilized Shark Teeth:

With every rain, more 65-million-year-old choppers wash out of the rocks in western Kansas.

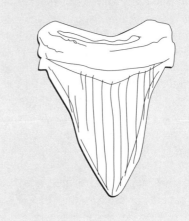

kansas when...

...your house lot cost absolutely nothing

Compared to Tokyo or California, land in Kansas is dirt cheap. In nine Kansas cities (okay, so they actually qualify as small towns), a new home lot can be picked up for a song. And you don't even have to sing in tune. In fact, you don't have to sing at all.

All you must do is agree to build a new house. Several of these free-lot-offering towns will even throw in a one-year family swimming pass at the local pool, free utility hookups, and $3,000 toward your down payment for every kid you can enroll in the public school system.

Minneapolis, Atwood, Plainville, Lincoln, Marquette, and most of the towns in Ellsworth County are among those that have taken this drastic step. Marquette gave away all 80 of its first batch of free lots in less than a year, boosting its population to 620.

Steve Piper, mayor of Marquette, says that the possibility of losing the local elementary school forced the community to act. In addition to giving away plots, residents cleaned up the downtown area, built a motorcycle museum, and began promoting tourism.

"I guess we're so stubborn that we're not going to let our town die," Piper says. "Instead of wasting money trolling for a major employer, we're going to build one family at a time."

Free (Zilch, Nada):

The going price for a new home lot in several Kansas towns.

... a ghost town has two wildly successful fried chicken restaurants

Less than 100 yards from each other in a virtual ghost town are not one but two popular fried chicken restaurants that together seat more than 800 people. They've been wildly successful for more than six decades.

Chicken Annie (aka Ann Frances Rehak Pichler) and Chicken Mary (aka Mary Zerngast) both started frying chicken in their homes when their coal mining hubbies lost their jobs. Annie's husband, Charles, lost his leg in March of 1933 in a coal car accident. Since the mining companies couldn't use an amputee, Annie, who had three small children at home, was forced to think quickly. She opened her three-room home to Charles's former coworkers, who gladly paid 15 cents for a mug of home brew and a ham or veal sandwich. By 1934 Annie was serving three pieces of fried chicken, German potato salad, German cole slaw with garlic, green peppers, a tomato slice, and bread for a whopping 75 cents.

In 1941 Chicken Mary, who lived across the street, had a similar string of bad luck when her husband, Joe, came down with a strange illness that caused him to lose his job. She, too, opened her kitchen table and began attracting coal miners, who would knock on the door any time, night or day, to

Fried Chicken:

A Kansas delicacy for which folks are willing to drive.

hustle a meal. Within four years Mary and Joe moved a pool hall they'd picked up cheap from a nearby mining camp to the lot next to their home. Although they originally called their pool-hall-turned-restaurant Joe's Place, it soon became known far and wide as Chicken Mary's because Mary, who was 5 feet, 1 inch tall and just about as wide, was a real character.

Today the chicken ladies' kids and grandkids run the restaurants.

you know you're in
kansas when...
... the enemy has changed, but the fort hasn't

If you saw *Dances with Wolves* (and who didn't?), you know that the movie opened in Kansas, at Fort Hays to be exact, where Kevin Costner's character was stationed before being sent to the abandoned Fort Sedgwick, also in Kansas. At one time Kansas had 27 military forts. Some were built to protect westward-bound settlers from Indians, others to protect Indians from westward-bound settlers.

Five of the forts have excellent museums, two are National Historic Sites, and two are still in use, although the enemies are no longer Indians and Confederates. Fort Riley, where George Custer was once stationed, supports the 1st Infantry Division, known as the "Big Red One." Fort Leavenworth, the oldest continuously operated army fort west of the Mississippi, supports the 35th Infantry Division. From there you can travel the Frontier Military Scenic Byway, a two-lane road that follows the old military trail between Fort Leavenworth and Fort Scott.

My favorite attraction at the military forts is the grave site of Chief, the last cavalry horse. When Chief kicked the bucket in 1968, the army gave him a proper burial with full military honors. The color guard showed up, the commanding general gave a speech, and a cavalry band played such military hits as "Hit the Leather," "Block Horse Troop," and "Sabre and Spurs."

Frontier Military Scenic Byway:

A 167-mile, mostly two-lane road along the old military trail used by the army to transport troops and supplies between Fort Leavenworth and Fort Scott.

They even buried him standing straight up with full military tack, including blanket rolls, canteen, and rifle. The proud bay gelding's burial site is at Fort Riley, across the parade field from the U.S. Cavalry Museum.

you know you're in
kansas when...
...you have your own state game show

The reality show *The Will*, which was filmed in Sedan, Kansas, came to an abrupt halt when CBS yanked it after one lowly Saturday-night showing. Ten contestants competing for the Kansas ranch of Bill Long, a millionaire businessman, managed to attract a measly 4.27 million viewers, making *The Will* the lowest-rated prime-time show of January 2005.

Maybe CBS should have scheduled *Go Kansas!* instead. Invented by Marci Penner and the Kansas Sampler Foundation, *Go Kansas!* is a wacky traveling game show played with a board—well, actually a 12- by 7-foot quilt, hand-stitched by Marci's mom and her sisters, that hangs on a PVC pipe frame. The game includes Kanna White (I'm told she's a cousin to Vanna) and 40 questions, 5 in each of these categories: architecture, art, commerce, cuisine, customs, geography, history, and people. As in *Jeopardy*, the questions get harder as you go down the board.

Penner (aka Alice Trabek and Patricia Sajak) presents the show some 30 times a year, including the annual playoffs at the Kansas State Fair. There are buzzers, chaser lights, scorekeepers, and a buzzer-turner-offer. Teams vie for points, and when they answer incorrectly, the question is submitted to the studio audience.

"People love it. Some take it really serious," Penner says. "We've had contestants demand a rematch, and one guy dressed in a suit was very earnest and would say, 'I'd like customs for 50, please.'"

Go Kansas!:

A traveling game show with all the drama and excitement of *Jeopardy*.

GO KANSAS!

you know you're in
kansas when...

...Handel's *Messiah* has been performed every Easter for more than 120 years

Lindsborg, a town in central Kansas with barely 3,000 residents, hasn't missed an Easter performance of Handel's *Messiah* since 1882. That was the year when Alma Swensson, wife of Carl Swensson, the new pastor at Bethany Lutheran Church, rounded up 75 local farmers, housewives, and shopkeepers to perform the famous oratorio that Handel wrote in 1741.

Rev. Swensson had seen *Messiah* performed in Illinois and decided it would be a fitting choice for his newly formed Bethany Oratorio Society. Never you mind that they didn't have a piano and had to use a tuning fork, or that Mrs. Swensson was left with no choice but to sing one of the soprano solos herself.

The chorus has grown a bit (there are now more than 300 volunteer singers, along with a 50-piece orchestra) and improved considerably since that first choir of farmers and shopkeepers. In fact, the Bethany Oratorio Society has become so renowned that its performance has been nationally televised more than a few times, and the group has performed at Carnegie Hall.

Handel's *Messiah:*

A Kansas musical tradition for 120-plus years.

...universities conduct performance tests on sunflowers

Performance tests on *sunflowers?* What else would you expect from a place that's known as the Sunflower State and that has its own Sunflower Commission? In case you're unfamiliar with the stellar board, the Sunflower Commission is a government-appointed body that regulates and develops policy for sunflowers and their accompanying commodities.

The Kansas Agricultural Experiment Station at Kansas State University conducts yearly performance tests on the state flower to find out which hybrids (there are more than 60 sunflower varieties), which types of soil (fallow, dry, or irrigated), and which conditions produce the best oilseed and confectionary products. In 2004, for example, seven test sites were used—and, yes, the performance test ended with ratings, tables, and diagrams.

Although the commission has been around for only a short time (2002 was its launch year), Kansans have been writing poems about the tall yellow plants and collecting sunflower items for decades. Bill Nicks, director of the Lenexa Parks and Recreation department, displays his collection (which he calls the world's largest; his wife calls it the world's onliest) in his office in the Lenexa Community Building. "My wife is scared to death I'll bring it home," he jokes.

It would take an awful lot of trips. At last count, Nicks had acquired 2,573 sunflower items, ranging from a 70-pound engraved manhole cover ("I can't divulge where I acquired this piece, but I will say I wouldn't advise jogging in Topeka at night," he says) to a sunflower-shaped flyswatter.

Since he started the collection in 1988, Nicks has blossomed into quite a sunflower celebrity. He has appeared on a General Mills billboard, in *Smithsonian* magazine, and on live remotes for the F/X Collectibles channel. One of his most unique items is the sheet music to the 1949 *Billboard* chart topper "Sunflower," which at one time or another was sung by Frank Sinatra, Bing Crosby, and 22 other artists.

Helianthus Annuus:

The scientific name of the Kansas state flower.

you know you're in
kansas when...
...farm fields are turned into public art

Most artists use easels, canvas, and paint. Stan Herd, an internationally known crop artist, uses corn fields, tractors, and organic materials to create his beautiful, oversize artwork. He forms living, growing crops into designs so huge that you can view them only from the air. A field near Atchison, for example, features a one-acre portrait of Amelia Earhart made entirely from perennial grasses.

Herd, who was born in tiny Protection, Kansas, and now lives in Lawrence, has sculpted famous crop art everywhere from Cuba to Manhattan's Upper West Side (*New York Countryside* was built along the Hudson River with gravel from the old Penn Square Railroad station and the help of three homeless men). But it was on the large farm fields of Kansas that he perfected his craft.

When millionaire Steve Fossett left Salina Regional Airport in March 2005 on a record-setting flight, he got a good look at a one-and-a-half-acre image of a glider made of dirt, tilled soil, and peat moss. Herd based it on a sketch by early aviation visionary Leonardo da Vinci. A few years earlier, Herd had used a Salina farm field to create a one-acre portrait of early environmentalist Aldo Leopold.

Herd, Stan:

Visionary Kansas crop artist.

Among other things, Herd has masterminded a portrait of Kiowa Indian chief Santana out of squash, melons, corn, and beans; a 160-acre portrait of Will Rogers; a giant Absolut Vodka bottle the size of 16 football fields that was featured in magazine ads for the Swedish import; and a 30-acre quilt pattern that was used in singer Michael Martin Murphy's music video for "A Long Line of Love."

you know you're in
kansas when...
...the whole country knows the words to your state song

Brewster Higley, who wrote the words to "Home on the Range," was a skillful physician before he moved to Kansas. After losing four wives (three died, and the fourth . . . well, let's just say that the marriage drove him to drink), Higley deserted his native Ohio, sent his kids to live with a relative in Illinois, and moved to a quiet log cabin on the banks of Beaver Creek.

Within months of moving to Smith County, he penned the poem "My Western Home." Some say he was inspired by the beauty of the Kansas prairie; others think Higley was just so relieved to be rid of Mercy Ann McPherson (wife #4) that his soul couldn't help but burst forth in poetic verse. A few others think the bottle might have egged on his creative impulses.

Either way, the poem was put to music two years later by Daniel E. Kelly, a carpenter from Smith County and violinist in the Harlan Brothers Orchestra. Kelly's sister-in-law, Virgie, kept the violin he wrote it on and, after the violin was ruined by rain, turned it into a trinket box decorated with ivory and mother of pearl.

The song became a popular hit across America and was performed by everyone from Gene Autry to Frank Sinatra. In 1933 President Franklin Roosevelt said it was his favorite song. As for Higley, he did get married again, to a Kansas girl named Sarah Clemens.

"Home on the Range":

1. The state song of Kansas. 2. FDR's favorite tune. 3. The one song besides "Itsy-Bitsy Spider" that every fourth grader in America can sing.

you know you're in
kansas when...
...you're standing over the largest gas field in North America

The Hugoton Gas Field in southwest Kansas is five times bigger than the state of Rhode Island. Since its discovery in 1927, it has produced trillions of cubic feet of natural gas, and it was an important player in World War I and both the Korean and Vietnam Wars. In fact, Bob Dole got the area recognized as an important contributor to America's energy security in Senate Resolutions 105 and 259.

Sixty-five million years ago, when the earth's crust was rumbling and roaring, pushing up the Rocky Mountains, Kansas was left with an abundance of natural gas and oil. Not a bad geological tradeoff, when you think about it. Colorado gets Marla Maples in Bogner; we get enough natural gas to heat every home in the state for at least 364 years.

Natural gas that forms between layers of chalk, shale, limestone, and sandstone is often accompanied by helium. Sure enough, the Hugoton Gas Field also contains the world's largest reserve of helium, accounting for nearly 60 percent of all helium used in the United States.

Hugoton Gas Field:

Named after the town of Hugoton, this gigantic field of natural gas runs under 13 counties in southwest Kansas.

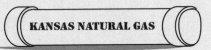

KANSAS NATURAL GAS

you know you're in
kansas when...
...34 is a lucky number

Not only was Kansas the 34th state to enter the union (January 29, 1861), but its favorite son, Dwight D. Eisenhower, was the 34th president of the United States, and its state flag features 34 stars.

Although Eisenhower was born in Denison, Texas, his family wised up quickly and moved to Kansas when he was but a babe. His mother was a pacifist (you might be, too, if you had seven sons), yet Eisenhower's dream was to serve in the military. And he did, graduating from West Point in 1915 and serving as a military aide to Generals Pershing and MacArthur. During World War II Eisenhower became the go-to guy, a commanding general of the victorious forces in Europe.

Ike, as he was known, returned home in 1945, a national hero. President Truman begged Ike to join him on the 1948 Democratic ticket, with Ike as president and Truman stepping down to VP. Eisenhower accepted the presidency of Columbia University instead.

It wasn't until 1952, while he was living in Paris and serving as supreme commander of the newly formed North Atlantic Treaty Organization (NATO), that Ike was finally persuaded to run for president—this time on the Republican ticket. He won hands-down.

Interestingly enough, the great military legend sent combat troops into action only once—in Lebanon in 1958. And, unlike recent Republican presidents, he believed in cutting defense spending and warned of the dangers of an unchecked military-industrial complex. As he so wisely said, "Every gun that is made, every warship launched, every rocket fired, signifies in the final sense a theft from those who hunger and are not fed, those who are cold and are not clothed."

Within six months of taking office, Eisenhower ended the Korean War and worked actively to ease the tensions of the Cold War.

I Like Ike:

Popular campaign slogan of the 34th president, the first to have a televised press conference, the first to have a heart attack in office, and the first to serve while both houses were controlled by the opposite party.

47

Rio de Janeiro has Carnivale; New Orleans has Mardis Gras. Liberal, Kansas, celebrates the day before Ash Wednesday with a 415-yard pancake-flipping race. And it's not just any race. It's an international battle between the women of Liberal and the women of Olney, England, followed 20 minutes later by a transatlantic phone call to see who won.

Liberal has been in on pre-Lenten hotcake-flipping since 1950. But legend has it that the women of England started back in 1445, when a member of St. Peter's and Paul's Church in Olney got so caught up making pancakes that she nearly missed the Shrove Tuesday service. Hurriedly trying to use up cooking fats (which were forbidden during Lent), the tardy penitent heard the church bell. Still clad in an apron, with the frying pan in hand, she raced to church, flipping away. The next year neighbors challenged her to a race that to this day runs from the town pump to the church steps.

In 1949 the president of the Liberal Jaycees got wind of the pancake race and wrote a letter to Ronald Collins, the vicar of Olney, challenging him to an international competition. On February 21, 1950, the first International Pancake Race was staged. It has been held every year since, attracting thousands of visitors and scads of media atten-tion—so much, in fact, that the 1980 race was declared a tie when a television news truck inadvertently blocked the finish line in Olney.

Modern rules state that the pancakes must be flipped once at the starting gate and once at the finish line. The winner receives a "kiss of peace," not to mention all that glory.

International Pancake Race:

A quarter-mile race that pits apron-wearing, skillet-carrying women in Liberal against apron-wearing, skillet-carrying women in Olney, England.

If you called somebody a *jayhawk* in 1848, when the name was first coined, they might not have spoken to you for days. Back then, it was anything but a compliment. The mythical bird, written about in newspapers around the country, was a cross between a noisy, quarrelsome blue jay and a stealthy sparrow hawk. In other words, you wouldn't dare turn your back on it.

In the 1850s, when Kansas was a battle-ground between those wanting slavery and those committed to a free state, the two competing factions looted, sacked, rustled cattle, stole horses, and basically wreaked havoc on each other's settlements. For a while, ruffians on both sides were called Jayhawkers, but the name eventually stuck to the Free Staters. Lawrence, where the University of Kansas would be founded, was a Free State stronghold.

During the Civil War, the jayhawk's unsavory reputation faded and it became a patriotic symbol. Governor Charles Robinson even raised a regiment called the Independent Mounted Kansas Jayhawks. By the time General Lee finally surrendered his Confederate troops to end the Civil War, jayhawks were synonymous with the impassioned people who made Kansas a free state.

Jayhawk:

1. A mythical bird you don't want to mess with. 2. The University of Kansas mascot.

When Kansas University football players first took the field in 1890, it seemed only natural to call them Jayhawkers. Over the years, student cartoonists have given the mascot many forms (including a ducklike hawk and an early bird with shoes for kicking opponents), but it was Harold D. Sandy's 1946 design of a smiling jayhawk that finally stuck. It was copyrighted in 1947.

In Tchaikovsky's classic Christmas ballet, the set opens with these words: "Once upon a time in Germany . . ." But in Kansas, the holiday ballet begins at a barn dance in Lawrence.

The Stahlbaum family celebrates the Christmas of 1854 with dozens of guests—some touting slavery and others (such as the notorious John Brown) fervently opposing it. The family is determined to enjoy Christmas without the interference of politics, so Herr Drosselmeyer, the children's godfather, presents them with life-size dolls, ducks, clowns, and mechanical monkeys.

Clara Stahlbaum, of course, gets a mysterious nutcracker that ends up broken and then repaired. It later takes her on a journey through Kansas, where she encounters blizzards, Native Americans, cavalry officers, and slavery advocates who attempt to burn down her family's barn.

In Kansas a mandolin orchestra plays Tchaikovsky's famous melodies, snakes and grasshoppers perform the dances, and the story line that could get a bit confusing in the original (where did that Sugar Plum Fairy come from, anyway?) is easy to follow, yet just as magical.

The Kansas *Nutcracker:*

Tchaikovsky's classic ballet score recomposed and danced to a Kansas legend.

you know you're in
kansas when...
...the wind speaks your name

Like many states, Kansas was named for the Indians who once lived there. The Kanza, known as the People of the South Wind, lived along the lower Kansas River in villages made of conical-shaped huts. They did a little farming and, like many Plains tribes, depended primarily on buffalo hunting.

The Kanza went on vision quests and consulted the wind before making important decisions. They believed that the wind carried messages to and from their allies, conducted reconnaissance missions on their enemies, knew the movement of buffalo, and led them to areas rich in nuts, fruits, and grain. To this day, descendants of the Kanza consult the south wind before going to court, choosing a new home, or signing necessary business papers.

Charles Curtis, the great-great-grandson of Kanza chief White Plume, was vice president of the United States under Herbert Hoover. He is the only vice president of Native American heritage and the only Kansan so far to hold that office. Curtis also served in the U.S. House of Representatives from 1903 to 1908 and in the Senate from 1909 to 1913 and 1915 to 1929. He was

born in North Topeka and raised both there and on the Kaw (another name for the Kanza tribe) Indian Reservation in Morris County.

William Mehojah, the last full-blooded Kanza, died April 23, 2000, and was buried in Omaha, Nebraska.

Kanza:

A once-proud Indian tribe that lives today in the hearts, the memories, and the gratitude of the people of Kansas.

you know you're in
kansas when...
...it takes three hours to go to the store

If you're really in a rush—say you want to get back home to watch *Desperate House-wives* by 8:00 P.M.— it's wise to park in the back and sneak in, maybe even wear a mask to hide your face. Otherwise, you'll have to stop and talk to everyone in town. They'll want to know what color your cousin chose for her prom dress and whether your neighbor ever heard back from that siding salesman. And even with the mask, they'll likely recognize your shoes.

The friendliness of Kansans sometimes jolts foreigners, such as Internet daters visiting from the East Coast. They're surprised when the owner of every car on the highway waves. Who *are* these people?

They're also not used to walking into the post office or a convenience store or a McDonald's and having a total stranger ask, "How are you today?" It throws them for a loop. When Kansans try this phrase (accompanied by a toothy grin) in Boston or Los Angeles, people assume they've just escaped from a small room with bars on the window.

Kindness of Strangers:

A phrase used to describe the outward kindness of Kansans, particularly to people outside the Midwest.

you know you're in
kansas when...
... the Christmas parade features farm machinery

The fact that the annual Kingman Christmas Parade shows off balers, tractors, combines, and other farm implements is not its most unusual feature. What makes the parade so unique is that it takes place at night (99.9 percent of all small-town parades take place before the noon bean or pancake feed), with all the floats (er, the combines and tractors) done up in showy Christmas lights. On parade night, the seat of this central Kansas county looks more like Las Vegas Boulevard than a town of barely more than 3,000 residents.

Of course, that's not to say you have to wait until it gets dark to take part in the festivities. This event, which takes place the first Saturday in December, kicks off with Breakfast with Santa and includes a 2-mile run, free matinees for kids, moving window displays, and so much daytime frivolity that some of the wee ones are sound asleep by the time the first John Deere, in all its lighted glory, rumbles down Main Street.

Kingman Christmas Parade:

The world's most unusual parade.

you know you're in
kansas when...
...a museum drives by with the world's largest collection of the world's smallest versions of the world's largest things

That's quite a mouthful, I admit, so let me break it down for you. The curator of this one-of-a-kind rolling museum is Erika Nelson, an artist who retired from jobs as a graphic designer and university instructor and settled in Lucas, Kansas, to pursue her true love: being the foremost expert on the world's largest things.

To earn this title, you have to know that the world's largest covered wagon is now a motorcycle repair shop and that, as of this writing, the world's largest kachina doll is up for sale for $400,000. You will then get to consult with chambers of commerce interested in building their own record-breaking things, those quintessential American icons that tourists stop to gawk at: the world's largest ball of string or the world's largest prairie dog or the world's largest hair ball, to name just a few that Kansas happens to tout.

Nelson toured to see all of these wonders, keeping meticulous notes and files. (She even wrote a thesis titled *Driving Around Looking at Big Things While Thinking About Spam*.) But Nelson wasn't content to just see them; she longed to duplicate them. Given that her van, a former senior-citizens' bus from Anderson County, Kansas, couldn't hold the world's largest steam shovels and talking cows, her best option was to make miniature replicas.

The smallest version of the world's largest ball of rubber bands, for example, is made of those tiny rubber bands used on braces. The world's smallest version of the world's largest otter is made from a dachshund figurine and modeling clay. Other exhibits in Nelson's rolling museum are the world's smallest versions of giant talking cows, doughnuts, bats, eight-balls, and badgers.

It was impossible to keep all that glory to herself, so Nelson was forced to open the museum. When she's not on tour, the van sits proudly in Lucas, Kansas.

Kitsch:

A whole career for Erika Nelson, whose fate was sealed at age three when her family visited Bemidji, Minnesota, to see the giant Paul Bunyan and Babe statues.

you know you're in
kansas when...

...people stay up all night playing bluegrass music

Every year, around mid-September, 20,000 or so campers converge on Winfield, Kansas, population 15,167. For five days and four nights, their only goal is to stay up as long as humanly possibly and soak up as much music (not to mention food and drink) as their tired, sunburned, bug-bitten bodies can tolerate.

The Walnut Valley Festival (that's the proper name, but everybody just calls it Winfield) is the national championship for just about every acoustic string instrument known to man—the flat-pick guitar, hammered dulcimer, banjo, fiddle, and mandolin, to name a few. Four stages feature nonstop entertainment from dawn to after midnight.

Of course, after midnight is when the real fun begins. Over in the Pecan Grove—among thousands of tents, sleeping bags, and pop-up campers—coffee is brewed so that the citizens of the night, regardless of age or physical condition, can stay awake and wander. The music changes as they move from campsite to campsite. Folk songs blend into Irish ballads. An old sea chantey might be played on a penny whistle. In the distance is the sound of a bagpipe, and somebody always brings a beat-up trumpet to play taps (funny at first, annoying by 4:00 A.M.). The crackling of campfires, the smell of wood smoke, and the laughter of friends are ever-present.

Land Rush:

A mad-dash run for the best camping spot at the venerable Walnut Valley Festival. Thousands of people arrive up to three weeks early to stake their claim.

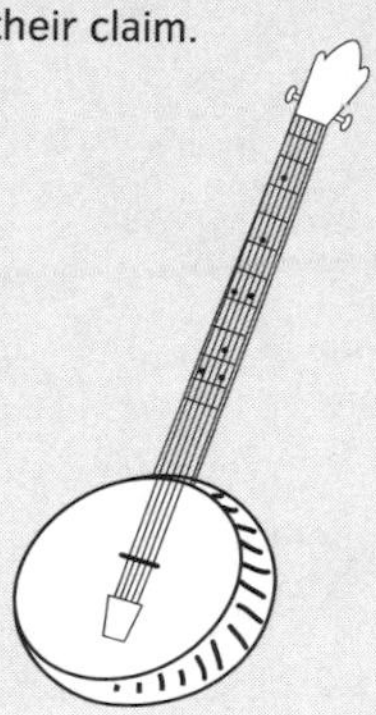

Campsites, elaborate locales with matching sofas and La-Z Boys, often have names—like the Blue Bayou, which always has a pond with an alligator or a turtle in it, and the Chicken Train Camp, which hosts chicken bingo, a clucking competition, and tie-dye Fridays (on which any camper can bring a T-shirt, a pair of underwear, or an old scarf for dye application).

One campsite throws a salsa competition, another has a Friday parade, and still another has a costume contest A recent winner was a *Wizard of Oz* Dorothy who sported tattoos from head to toe.

55

you know you're in
kansas when...
... wheat is considered an art medium

Have you priced paint and canvas lately? No wonder the words *starving* and *artist* so often go hand in hand. But in Kansas, anyone with a bathtub and a stalk of wheat can become an artist. Kansas's 28,500 wheat farmers produce more than 374 million bushels of the grain a year (more than any other state in the country), and most residents have bathtubs—so it's no big surprise that they weave wheat the way other folks knit yarn.

All you do is take a few stalks of wheat, soak them until they are pliable, and start braiding. I've seen wheat woven into earrings, Christmas ornaments, wreaths, wind mills, door hangings, witches, barns, and even a 5-foot-tall doll wearing a pioneer dress. The Kansas State Fair has a competition each September for the year's most original and beautiful wheat weavings.

For the bicentennial, the Smithsonian Institution commissioned twins in Goessel to weave a life-size replica of the Liberty Bell out of Turkey Red wheat, the variety that put Kansas on the map. Marie and Martha Voth spent 2,000 hours creating the straw bell that, after its stint in the Smithsonian, is now back in Kansas at Newton's Turkey Red Wheat Palace.

The Last Straw:

What artists in Kansas use to be creative.

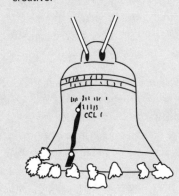

Although the popular TV series *Little House on the Prairie* lasted nine seasons (1974–1983), Laura Ingalls Wilder lived in Kansas for only one year. When her pa built a tiny, one-room log cabin near Independence, it was the 89th residence in Rutland Township. But not 15 months later, Laura's family learned that they'd mistakenly built on the Osage Indian Reservation. They moved back to Wisconsin, never knowing that six months later the land where they'd met Mr. Edwards and Dr. Tann was officially opened to homesteaders.

Nonetheless, the story set in Kansas remains the most popular of Wilder's nine books, with five million copies sold. The Little House—a 14- by 16-foot cabin—has been authentically recreated in the very spot where it once stood. There's also a well that Pa and Mr. Scott dug; Sunny Side School, the 1871 schoolhouse that Laura would have attended, had she been old enough; and a post office where she might have sent a letter, had she known how to write back then.

Little House on the Prairie:

If it were still standing, the "little house" that Laura Ingalls Wilder wrote about would be in Wayside (if it were still a town).

Kansas has more Statues of Liberty than New York. Twenty-six, in fact, were erected between 1949 and 1951 by Boy Scout troops around the state that were able to raise $350, the price at that time for an 8-foot, 4-inch Lady Liberty.

Jack Whitaker, a Kansas City businessman and Boy Scout commissioner, hatched the scheme for the miniature sisters of liberty to celebrate the Scouts' 40th-anniversary theme, "Strengthen the Arm of Freedom." Whitaker contracted a Chicago factory to churn out the 290-pound stamped copper statues, and before he knew it, Kansas troops had put them up in parks, school grounds, courthouses, town squares, museums, and city halls across the state.

Kansas wasn't alone. In all, more than 200 little sisters were erected in the United States, two U.S. protectorates, and two other countries. After September 11, 2001, Save Outdoor Sculpture—a joint project of Heritage Preservation and the Smithsonian—decided to have a second look at the statues. Needless to say, 50 years of weather and vandalism had taken their toll, and some of the statues had been put in storage or sold for scrap.

So far, 100 of the original statues have been accounted for. And thanks to patriotism fostered by 9/11, communities around

Little Sisters of Liberty:

Two hundred clones of the big mama in New York were erected in 39 U.S. states, Panama, the Philippines, Guam, and Puerto Rico. Kansas, however, erected the most.

Kansas have rallied to restore their symbols of American pride. St. John honored its refurbished Miss Liberty with a parade, patriotic speeches, and a banquet; Leavenworth issued a special postmark to commemorate a rededication ceremony for its statue.

Plug "Long Branch Saloon" into Google, and you'll quickly discover that there's not a state among us that doesn't have at least one. There's one in North Carolina that hosts leprechaun wrestling every St. Patty's Day. Berkeley, California, had one in the heady 1960s that featured all sorts of revolutionary bands, from Asleep at the Wheel to Country Joe and the Fish.

But the original Long Branch Saloon—the one that has inspired the name at clubs as far away as Malaysia—was located right in the heart of Dodge City, which was called everything from "hell on the plain" to the "wickedest city in America." In the 1870s soldiers at Fort Dodge and local cowboys waged a bet over a baseball game. The soldiers, prompted by a few brewskies, agreed that if they lost the game, they'd provide the building materials for a saloon. (Anything to get them out of the hot Kansas sun.) Luckily for all, the soldiers went on to lose the game and remained true to their word.

Chalk Beason bought the Long Branch in 1878 and used it as the venue for his world-famous Dodge City Cow-Boy Band. This brass ensemble, led by a conductor keeping time with a pearl-handled six-shooter, had gigs at Madison Square Garden, the Chicago World's Fair, and Benjamin Harrison's presidential inauguration in 1889.

Why else might "Long Branch Saloon" be the name preferred by 2 out of 10 bar owners? It's where Marshall Matt Dillon, Miss Kitty, Doc, and the rest of Dodge City hung out during *Gunsmoke*, the longest-running TV western in celluloid history. The show lasted for 20 years and 635 episodes before it bit the trail dust in 1975.

Long Branch Saloon:

1. Popular name for a watering hole.
2. Historic bar in Dodge City. 3. The main set for *Gunsmoke*, in which good triumphed over evil every 60 minutes, with only a few commercial interruptions.

Most towns with a population of 427 are lucky to have a gas station, let alone a museum. But Lucas, an anything-but-sleepy town in north-central Kansas, has five major museums, attracts scads of international visitors, and is probably the most interesting locale in the state.

Especially if you like grassroots art. Also called outsider art and primitive art (and yes, "downright bizarre" by some people), this genre thrives in Kansas, which has more grassroots artists per capita than any other state.

The Lucas legacy began in 1907, when S. P. Dinsmoor, a retired farmer, nurse, and Civil War veteran, began building a concrete Garden of Eden there. When all was said and done, Dinsmoor had used 113 tons of cement to sculpt grape arbors, 40-foot trees, a life-size Adam and Eve, a devil whose eyes light up (he was the first in Logan to have electricity), and 100 other statues.

The Garden of Eden is one point of what locals call the Lucas Triangle. At the other points are the Florence Deeble Rock Garden, whose namesake, a retired English and history teacher, created giant concrete postcards of Mount Rushmore, the Grand Tetons, and other places that she visited; and the Grassroots Arts Center, a fascinating three-building museum with art made from everything from grapefruit peels and dried chewing gum to empty Milk of Magnesia bottles.

Also worth visiting are the World's Largest Collection of the World's Smallest Versions of the World's Largest Things Traveling Roadside Museum (see the Kitsch entry) and Mri Pilar's Garden of Isis Starclock, part of the Deeble House.

The Lucas Triangle:

Mecca for anyone interested in grassroots arts.

If you're searching for the perfect plate of *vareniki,* try the Kansas Mennonite Relief Sale, the largest event at the state fairgrounds (besides the state fair itself, of course) in Hutchison. Thousands come from miles around to eat Mennonite and Amish dishes such as *vareniki,* fried or boiled dough (often stuffed with cottage cheese curd and topped with ham gravy); *moos,* a dessert soup made from dried fruit; and *bohne beroggi,* a sweet yeast bread with pinto beans and cream sauce.

The annual two-day sale is the second largest Mennonite Relief Sale in the country. Not a big surprise, given that central Kansas towns like Inman, Buhler, Goessel, Newton, Hillsboro, and Moundridge were all settled by German and Russian Mennonites. Starting in 1874, hundreds of these immigrants came to Kansas after their 100-year-old immunity from religious persecution was threatened. They chose land in Marion, Harvey, McPherson, and other nearby counties for several reasons. First, the government exempted them from military service and gave them the right to speak German. Second, the landscape resembled the treeless south Russian countryside that some of them had left behind. The Santa Fe Railroad recruited these newcomers with massive advertising campaigns.

Mennonites:

1. A denomination of Pacifists, first organized in Holland, who immigrated to Kansas via Germany, Russia, and Switzerland. 2. The creators of some odd but delicious foods.

Vareniki
2 cups flour
1 teaspoon salt

The Relief Sale raises more than $300,000 for the Mennonite Central Committee, a worldwide relief organization formed in 1920. More than 70 Mennonite, Brethren in Christ, and Amish congregations donate gifts and services for the festival and benefit auction. Shoppers can buy everything from hand-crafted furniture and quilts (more than 250 quilting circles donate their creations) to restored antique tractors.

you know you're in
kansas when...
...hurricanes are a nightly occurrence

You can find hurricanes—yes, hurricanes, those fierce tropical storms characterized by heavy winds and driving rain—in Kansas every night at exactly 10:00 P.M. That's when the Sandbar, a cozy cabana in downtown Lawrence, sponsors the only indoor hurricane in the world.

Complete with a phony newscast and Hollywood-worthy special effects, the hurricane makes it impossible to do anything but drink margaritas or Bahama Mamas and weather the storm for a full 15 minutes. It involves fog machines, loud theme music, simulated lightning, and live mermaids dancing on the bar.

A favorite of visiting alumni from the University of Kansas (which is within walking distance), the Sandbar features huge tanks of exotic fish, tropical decor, a juke box with lots of songs that everyone knows by heart, and a gift shop with clever T-shirts and the bar's signature costume: bras made from coconuts (what else?). In fact, if you can come up with a unique logo to paint on the coconuts, you win your own set free of charge.

Mermaids:

At the Sandbar in Lawrence, patrons don mermaid costumes and dance on the bar while a hurricane rages.

you know you're in
kansas when...
... you're the butt of everyone else's joke

Like blondes and Michael Jackson, Kansans have long taken the brunt of national ribbing. We're what you might call the Rodney Dangerfield of states. In the national consciousness, it's widely accepted that Kansas is a synonym for drab, flat, and backward.

H. L. Mencken proclaimed Kansas the quintessential "cow state, chock-full of hayseeds, moralizers, and Methodists." In the James Bond film *Diamonds Are Forever,* the evildoers reject Kansas as a testing site for their anti-matter weapon because "the world wouldn't learn about it for a year." *Spy* magazine called Kansas the "boringest state in the union."

Obviously that writer, besides being functionally illiterate, never bothered to get off Interstate 70. Just because I-70 was the country's first section of interstate (completed soon after President Eisenhower signed the Interstate Highway Act of 1956), doesn't mean that's all there is to Kansas. I mean, c'mon, we have nine distinct physiographic regions ranging from the High Plains in the west and the Ozark Plateau in the east to the Red Hills and the Flint Hills in the center of our state.

As for being backward, all I can say is that Kansas was the first state to ratify the 15th Amendment, which gave African Americans the right to vote; the first to advocate a 40-hour workweek; and the first to push for pure food and drug laws. And Kansas women have been voting, holding office, and passing bills for going on two centuries.

Mistaken Identity:

When Colorado ski instructors look for examples of the quintessential rube, residents of the state next door are sure to come up.

you know you're in
kansas when...
...oysters don't come from the ocean

There's a popular appetizer here in Kansas called mountain oysters—an irony, given that we don't have an abundance of either mountains or oceans from which to find seafood. So where do these oysters come from? If you don't have a weak stomach or a closed mind, read on. (If you *are* squeamish, you'd better skip to the next entry.)

Mountain oysters—also known as prairie oysters, cowboy caviar, tendergroins, swinging beef, and calf fries—are calf testicles. Not everybody can appreciate this delicacy found on many Kansas menus and in even more deep freezers.

Eating animal genitalia dates back to ancient Roman times, when people believed that eating a healthy animal's organ corrected a deficiency in the person eating it. We do it in Kansas because . . . well, castration makes a calf more tender and his personality less obstinate. Besides that, the end result is quite tasty.

But before we stick these savories in our mouths, we skim them, wash them, roll them in flour and pepper, and fry them in a pan. Cowboys used to toss mountain oysters into the fire until they exploded, at which time they were considered ready to eat.

Mountain Oysters:

1. Calf testicles (not to be mistaken with bull testicles), which are roughly the size of a walnut. 2. A Kansas delicacy; also called gourmet gonads.

... your railroad station is modeled after William Shakespeare's home

The Amtrak station in Newton was modeled after the half-timbered home of a certain famous playwright born in Stratford-on-Avon, England, in 1564. William Shakespeare's father, John—a glove maker, wool dealer, and mayor of his prosperous city in central England—constructed the house on Henley Street in two stages.

It took the city of Newton only one stage to build the train station. It's not an exact clone, but it's pretty darn close. Erected by the Atchison, Topeka and Santa Fe Railroad in 1929–30, Shakespeare's look-alike was Newton's fourth railroad station. An earlier incarnation housed a popular Harvey Restaurant, complete with attractive Harvey girls. (These waitresses were made popular by that *other* Judy Garland film, *The Harvey Girls*.)

The fourth time was obviously the charm, because the Stratford-on-Avon version—which cost $350,000—still has nightly arrivals and departures, an Amtrak ticket office, and classrooms for the local branch of Hutchinson Community College. The brick-and-timber building is on both the state and national Registers of Historic Places.

Newton Train Station:

To be or not to be? That is not the question for this dramatic Amtrak station, which also serves as a community college.

you know you're in
kansas when...
...women go first

In 1888 an all-woman town council led by a female mayor was elected in Oskaloosa. This, I hasten to point out, was 32 years before women in the rest of the country could even vote. And Oskaloosa's mayor wasn't the first. Argonia had elected Susanna Salter, the first woman in the entire country to serve as mayor, a year earlier.

Town drunks thought it would be funny to put Salter, who was head of Argonia's Temperance Committee, on the ballot. She was elected by two-thirds of the town voters, a joke that backfired on her nominating committee. The first things Salter did were ban the sale of alcohol and close down Argonia's bars.

Other Kansas women have gone on to be "firsts," including Amelia Earhart, the first woman to fly solo across the Atlantic and coast to coast; Rena Milner, the first woman city manager; Mabel Chase, the first female county sheriff; Julia Archibald Holmes, the first woman to climb Pike's Peak; Lucy Hobbs Taylor, the first female dentist; Georgia Neese Clark Gray, the first female U.S. treasurer; and Lynette Woodard, the first woman to play for the Harlem Globetrotters.

Numero Uno:

1. A desirable ranking when it comes to achievement. 2. A fitting name for the many Kansas women who voted, held office, and forged careers before their counterparts in other states.

you know you're in
kansas when...
... half your tourist attractions are on dirt roads

Oh, okay, there are a couple attractions on Interstate 70, the highway that non-Kansans use to traverse our state. The Dwight D. Eisenhower Library and Museum in Abilene is only 2 miles south of I-70, and the Sternberg Museum of Natural History, with all its dinosaurs and sea monsters, is a mere mile from exit 159.

But lots of our natural wonders—Arikarae Breaks, Rock City, and Monument Rocks, to name just a few—can be accessed only by dirt roads. Mount Sunflower, the state's highest point, is in the middle of some cattle rancher's pasture.

To get close enough to take a picture of the Wee Kirk of the Valley, a tiny stone cathedral with statues of the Last Supper and Jesus in the Garden of Gethsemane, you have to climb over a barbed-wire fence and numerous cow patties. And that's after you've followed a gravel road 6.5 miles out of Cedar Vale. (I know, where's Cedar Vale?)

If Big Brutus, a coal shovel that draws 40,000 visitors a year (one of them being Brooke Shields), wasn't sixteen stories high, nobody would ever find it. It's miles from even a two-lane Kansas highway. Call it a small miracle that the gift shop is able to offer such a fine selection of souvenirs, including Big Brutus whistles, fans, Frisbees, cookbooks, and T-shirts.

Off the Beaten Path:

The location of many underpromoted Kansas landmarks.

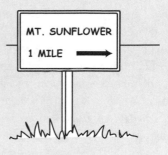

The world's largest buffalo, located atop a bluff on a 2,000-acre buffalo ranch, is a good 16 miles from the nearest interstate. Not necessarily a hindrance, except that there's nary a brochure advertising it and nary a sign with directions.

Suffice it to say that if Kansas landmarks were in any other state, they would be promoted with brochures, tour guides, and high-dollar Web sites, and paved highways would lead to the front gates. In fact, the only reason people think Kansas is flat and dull is because no one bothered to tell them otherwise.

The privy for the post office in Elk Falls is . . . well, it's an outhouse. And as far as postmaster Gloria Wolf knows, it's the only working outhouse still being used by the U.S. Postal Service, although she admits that she hasn't checked them all.

But, hey, it's private (Wolf is the only postal employee for the little town of 121), and except for the occasional times she forgets to stock up, there's plenty of toilet paper. (Corn cobs, she says, went out with hoop skirts.) The best deal of all is that the outhouse gets star billing in the town's annual Outhouse Tour, which takes place on the Saturday and Sunday before Thanksgiving. That's when Wolf decorates for company, putting a flag, a statue of Uncle Sam, and a poem that she wrote—something about "neither rain nor snow and the postman needing to go"—inside the outhouse.

The tour attracts hundreds of visitors to Elk Falls, known as the World's Largest Living Ghost Town. Joining Wolf's entry—the Priority Privy—are other outhouses that have their own witty names and elaborate features. They include the Gingerbread Outhouse, in which Hansel and Gretel's two seats are painted red and white, like peppermint candy; the Chamber Pot, an elaborate porcelain throne created by Steve Fry, the local potter; the Flower Pot, a former WPA outhouse that has been

redesigned and sits next to the local bed-and-breakfast's garden; the Nature Calls Outhouse, donated by the phone company, with a phone receiver rather than a moon cut out of the door and a little sign urging those who "have to go" to use the competitor's phonebooks first; and the Pooh Puppy Palace, designed around a fire hydrant.

Everyone who comes to town for the tour and buys a button gets a map and a ballot for voting.

Outhouse:

A toilet housed inside a rustic structure much too small and odiferous for lounging.

you know you're in
kansas when...
... bicyclists are called pancake riders

There's always a section of BAK—that's Biking Across Kansas, an annual bicycling event—that gets a bit flat. Some might even say tedious. But when the 800 to 900 participants each June get to said section, they pedal through it with lots of jokes, chief among them being their nickname: pancake riders.

The 500-mile, eight-day ride (pronounced "B-A-K," as in three separate letters, not "back") has been held since 1975. It starts in the western part of the state, where riders are more likely to find flat terrain, and proceeds east. By the end of the journey, most would gladly surrender their neon jerseys for a brief taste of those pancake spots they enjoyed along the route.

Contrary to popular belief, Kansas is not entirely flat, and the terrain on BAK can be downright challenging. There are often nefarious headwinds, the weather can be sticky, and, yes, it sometimes rains buckets. If that doesn't sound daunting enough, consider other Kansas bicycling races such as the Wicked Wind 100, sponsored by the

Pancake Riders:

Mistaken nickname for people who ride bikes in Kansas.

Oz Bicycle Club of Wichita; the Lizard Under the Skillet, sponsored by the Lawrence Bicycle Club; and the Kansas Survival Series, a seven-race contest that's not for the faint of heart.

...you learned to shoot a gun before you learned to multiply

Don't expect to find many Kansans watching football games on the second Saturday of November. Doesn't matter who the Jayhawks or the Wildcats are playing. It's the opener for pheasant season, and even hard-core gridiron addicts can be found tramping around in wooded creek bottoms, wearing camouflage. In fact, many of our 105,000 resident pheasant hunters actually believe that opening Saturday is a national holiday.

In some Kansas communities (such as Norton, which bills itself as the Pheasant Hunting Capital of the World), pheasant opener is the highlight of the year. Expect a party-like atmosphere, with hunters hosting pancake breakfasts, civic groups holding fundraising hunts, and local diners crowded with out-of-state pickups.

Kansas has the real deal when it comes to pheasants, unlike many eastern states that have slow, pen-raised game. (The Humane Society recently filed a lawsuit against Massachusetts for the practice of buying pheasants, trucking them to Cape Cod National Seashore, and releasing them before the October hunts.) The Kansas Department of Wildlife and Parks—with the help of rural mail carriers, wildlife biologists, and landowners—tracks pheasant numbers during August roadside counts for a forecast usually released a full two months

before the opener. Although it varies from season to season, the number of ring-necked roosters bagged in Kansas per season averages around 660,000.

That usually rings in at third in the nation, but keep in mind that Kansas has denser pheasant populations over larger areas than any other state (more than a million acres); a higher bag limit (four at last count); a longer season; and, in general, fewer days of extreme weather that might send hunters back to their hotel rooms.

Pheasant Opener:

The day when Kansas hunters are legally allowed to start bagging ring-necked pheasants.

you know you're in
kansas when...
... your Pizza Hut is the only one without a red roof

The Pizza Hut that sits on the campus of Wichita State University was the very first. Yes, the restaurant that literally changed how Americans eat was launched in a tiny brick building that used to be a bar.

It all started in 1958 when a fight broke out at that bar, which sat next to a Wichita grocery store owned by the widowed mother of Frank and Dan Carney. The landlord, fed up with noisy tenants, suggested to the elder Carney that her sons, who were students at the university, open a small, quiet restaurant there instead.

While mom sewed red-and-white-checked curtains, the Carney boys, ages 19 and 24, rounded up an old baby bathtub in which to mix dough for a popular new food called pizza. They named their restaurant Pizza Hut, mainly because that was all the letters they could fit on the sign used by the building's former occupant, the B&B Lounge.

Like many historic landmarks, the first Pizza Hut was almost torn down and turned into a parking lot. Luckily, Fran Jabara, a former dean of business at WSU, recognized the building's value and had it moved, brick by brick, from Bluff Street and Kellogg Drive to the university campus.

Pizza Hut:

This multinational corporation, started in Kansas, gave the world deep-dish and thin-crust pizza.

At first it looked like the landmark would get its proper due. Hundreds of people attended the dedication in 1986, including the president of PepsiCo (to which the Carneys sold their restaurant chain for a cool $300 million), and WSU's Center for Entrepreneurship claimed it as headquarters for budding entrepreneurs. But then the basement flooded. As far as anyone knows, the building hasn't been used for anything but storage since.

... summer nights sound exactly like they did before the Industrial Revolution

Friends in New York pity me. "Don't you miss the symphony, the art museums?" they lament, shaking their heads. I appreciate their concern, but when it comes to beautiful music, it's hard to beat a summer night on the Kansas prairie.

I'd pit my cicadas, my crickets, my frogs, and their courtship rituals against the New York Philharmonic any day. The Kansas wind blowing its many-voiced chorus through stands of buffalo grass wins hands-down against taxi horns, screeching brakes, and even *Seinfeld* reruns.

Summer nights in Kansas demand open windows with the same urgency as a picketing Teamster. Curtain-rustling breezes bring in the scent of honeysuckle, freshly turned earth, and the distant, familiar yelp of coyotes.

And as for the art museums, I've yet to see a Monet or Picasso that even comes close to a clear, cloudless night on the Kansas prairie. Miles from city lights, the stars overhead whisper to kids, "See if your mom will let you drag your mattress outside. Tell her you'll fall asleep counting."

Porch People:

People who eschew the sterile preoccupation with tightly sealed, air-conditioned homes, fluorescent skyscrapers, and other things artificial.

...people use 300-pound blocks of limestone to make fence posts

Though limestone has its merits, wood is obviously more practical when it comes to building things. It's about a thousand times lighter, doesn't take a whole team of horses to move from place to place, and makes a much hotter fire for cooking biscuits. But when early settlers migrated to the Kansas prairies, there weren't a whole heck of a lot of trees. They solved the campfire/biscuit dilemma with bison chips. But despite the ample supply, most pioneers didn't relish the idea of building permanent homes with buffalo doo-doo.

The ever-ingenious pioneers opted for sod instead . . . until they discovered that in most of north-central Kansas, an 8- to 12-inch layer of limestone rested only a few feet under the soil. They used blocks of limestone (which, I don't have to tell you, weren't exactly a piece of cake to quarry) to build not only homes but also clotheslines, hitching posts, watering troughs, well covers, bridges, tombstones, churches, schools, county courthouses, and fence posts. The latter inspired the common name for Kansas limestone: post rock limestone.

Although rock fence posts went out in the 1920s, more than 40,000 miles of the old post rock fences remain standing in north-central Kansas. And there's still a prolific supply of limestone, which sculptors now

Post Rock Limestone:

A sturdy building material in north-central Kansas. Wood fence posts last an average of six years; those made from limestone have survived since the late 1800s.

use to chisel such things as benches, bird baths, sundials, and even shelves.

The late Inez Marshall, a former truck driver, auto mechanic, and traveling evangelist from Portis, sculpted Model Ts, a full-size motorcycle, a 500-pound Abraham Lincoln, and just about anything else you can think of out of post rock limestone. Even though she was partially disabled, Marshall managed to turn monstrous and very heavy pieces of limestone into a Last Supper sculpture; a Kennedy Table (a tribute to JFK, with dozens of Kennedy dollars embedded in it); and a miniature 11-room Sunshine Hospital that had doctors, an operating room, a nursery, and a dining hall complete with food on the tables.

you know you're in
kansas when...
...skyscrapers hold grain

Look off in the distance, in practically any direction, and you'll notice a grain elevator dominating the skyline. We call them *prairie skyscrapers*, and every town has at least one. In some cases, the grain elevator stands long after the town itself has been abandoned. Oftentimes, it's still being used.

Unpainted, weather-beaten, and windowless, grain elevators are often mistaken for useless relics. Like numerous things in Kansas, that's a disguise. During World War I they were so important that home guards were called in to protect them from suspected saboteurs. Come harvest time, wheat trucks line up for blocks, waiting for scale attendants to fill out weigh tickets that, in many ways, determine a farmer's upcoming year.

The term *elevator* is commonly used to describe the entire complex, which includes not only the elevator but also the driveway, ramps, and an office with a walkway and an annex. There's also a very large scale, big enough to weigh a semi.

Hutchinson's Grain Elevator J, one of the largest grain elevators in the world, holds 18 million bushels of wheat—enough to fill 5,400 railroad cars. One lap around the

Prairie Skyscrapers:

Another name for grain elevators, usually located along railroad tracks.

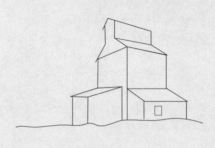

huge concrete structure makes an even mile. If you can run it in less than 3 minutes and 43 seconds, you'll beat the mile record set by Hicham El Guerrouj in 1999. In that case, maybe you should try out for the Olympics!

you know you're in
kansas when...
...symphony orchestras play Bach on the prairie

Sprawled on blankets or sitting on rocks amid milkweed, larkspur, bluestem, coreopsis, sunflowers, and other native plants, Kansas symphony aficionados enjoy Bach performed to the counterpoint of warbling prairie birds.

Jane Koger, who owns 4,000 acres in the Flint Hills near Matfield Green, started the tradition with "Symphony on the Prairie," a 60-piece, all-female orchestra that provided entertainment at her women-only cattle ranch. Almost 3,000 people showed up at the free 1994 event.

Since then, dozens of outdoor prairie symphonies have sprung up around Kansas, including an official outfit called Symphony on the Tallgrass Prairie Inc. that hosts outdoor concerts at different locations in the Flint Hills. The 2006 concert, for example, will be staged at the Tallgrass Prairie National Preserve, the only national park in Kansas.

The Winfield Regional Symphony often performs outdoors at the ranch of Dick and Dolly Bonfy, near Arkansas City. Along with the Paul Winter Consort, the PrairieFest Chorus, and the Prairie Wind Dancers, the Winfield Symphony hosted the world premier of *Carl Sandburg's Prairie* (by Eugene Friesen) on the Bonfy ranch stage in 2001.

Prairie Symphonies:

Where Bach and Beethoven mix with wildflowers and prairie grasses.

you know you're in
kansas when...
...road graders are standard government issue

Lots of county roads in Kansas are gravel. Meaning unpaved. With little rocks. Or mud when it happens to rain. License plates get so dirty that you can barely tell which county, let alone which state, a car is registered in. Driving would probably be treacherous if most roads weren't straighter than Pollyanna, allowing you to see every last bit of traffic—that is, one other car every hour or so—for miles in every direction.

Gravel roads save county governments lots of money on asphalt, but the one item that no county in Kansas can spare is a road grader—that crucial machine that keeps unpaved roads level. If you live in western Kansas, road graders are as common as tumbleweeds, sunflowers, and dead birds.

The dead birds, I should probably explain, are a direct result of the straight roads. Refusal to speed on roads this straight (at least the ones that *are* paved) is considered illegal. And when you're doing 85 or 90 miles per hour and a bird flies into your path... well, *Splat* with a capital S would probably be a good word to describe it. It's not a problem if you're in a Ford F-150, but if you're on a motorcycle, the collision can be pretty painful—not only for Kansas's kamikaze avians, but also for you.

Road Grader:

A large piece of heavy machinery that's a necessity in western Kansas.

you know you're in
kansas when...
...your college chant is sung at the Olympics

At the Olympic games in 1920, the King of Belgium requested a cheer from a typical American college. The assembled athletes quickly agreed that the Rock Chalk Chant from the University of Kansas was the most distinctive cheer in American college sports, and they proceeded to launch into a rousing rendition of the simple chant that has been likened to a Gregorian chant.

The chant dates back to 1866, when it was adopted by the university's science club. To pass the time on a train ride to Lawrence from Wichita, a chemistry professor named E. H. S. Bailey made up a cheer that matched the cadence of the train's wheels. At first, the cheer was "Rah, Rah, Jayhawk, KU" repeated three times.

An English professor later suggested "Rock Chalk" in place of "Rah, Rah" because the former rhymed with "Jayhawk" and because it was symbolic of the limestone, also known as chalk rock, surrounding Mount Oread. This version became the official university cheer in 1887.

It was used by Kansas troops fighting in the Philippines in 1899, in the Boxer Rebellion in China, and in World War II. Teddy Roosevelt pronounced the Rock Chalk Chant the greatest college chant he'd ever heard.

The words are deceivingly simple. The tone in which they are chanted and the distinctive cadence in which each verse is delivered are what make the cheer special. The best way to appreciate it is to sit in Allen Fieldhouse before a Missouri Tigers game.

Rock Chalk Chant:

A famous college sports chant, maybe the only one started for a science club. To wit, it was invented four years before KU even had a football team.

you know you're in
kansas when...
...a 19th-century mineral boom is still the biggest industry in town

California and Alaska had a gold rush. Colorado had a silver boom. In Kansas, we had a salt boom. It happened in 1887, soon after Ben Blanchard accidentally discovered salt near Hutchinson. He was hoping for oil.

Once the word got out that Kansas had the world's largest piece of salt—100 miles long by 40 miles wide—miners flooded to Hutch. At one time there were more than 26 salt companies there, producing up to 44.1 million tons of salt each year. Blocks of salt were cut whole from the 10- to 12-foot veins. The impact of the industry is evident today in business names like Salt City Land and Title and the Salt City Shuttle; the local high school mascot is even the Salt Hawk.

Hutch's salt boom came just in the nick of time. It saved the little town that had been started by a Baptist minister who had marked out the streets with buffalo skulls and threatened to reclaim the deed of any property owner who dared drink hard liquor or even carry it onto his land. Not a popular statute in the wild Kansas frontier.

Hutchinson is about to become the only town in the United States with a museum that is 650 feet below the ground. Exhibits in the soon-to-open Kansas Underground Salt Museum, a former salt mine, will explain the geological formation of salt, its uses throughout history, and the importance of local mines. In 1903, for example,

Salt:
1. A white, grainy substance used to season food, de-ice roads, and preserve meat and Egyptian mummies. 2. A Kansas commodity that could easily keep the world in margaritas for eternity.

the Interstate Commerce Commission (ICC) held a hearing in Hutchinson that pitted the "Trusts," nine companies under the owner of Morton Salt, against independent salt producers. The hearing led to the Elkins Act of 1903, which gave the ICC more power to regulate railroad transportation rates for commodities like salt.

The only things stored in some of the salt mines now are reels of classic Hollywood movies, which stay preserved in the mine's ideal temperatures.

you know you're in
kansas when...
... your bank doubles as a museum

Kansans like to joke that if they accidentally stepped into the wrong bank, the tellers and president—who likely have known them since the day they were born—would cash their checks anyway.

Some banks in Kansas do more than cash checks. Citizen State Bank in Morland doubles as the Floyd Riggs Comic Book Museum. It features 164 popular comic books from the 1940s and 50s, all carefully mounted and framed. And the First State Bank in Norton houses the Gallery of Also-Rans—as in former presidential hopefuls, victims of a well-known political rule of thumb: The winner gets the White House; the loser gets doomed to obscurity.

DeWitt Clinton, for example, was a mover and shaker who proposed the Erie Canal and swept the Republican nomination in 1812. But thank to James Madison, the Democrat who defeated him, his name can barely be recalled.

For years the Gallery of Also-Rans was more obscure than its subjects, hosting 30 or so visitors a year. But during the 2000 election *USA Today* got wind of it, and now the little museum makes for a popular national feature every four years.

W. W. Rouse, former president of the bank, started the museum after one of his daughters gave him a book by Irving Stone called

They Also Ran. Until his death in 1981, Rouse wrote a tribute to the losing candidates in presidential elections and requested their photos from the Library of Congress.

Now Diana McGee, secretary of the bank, serves as curator, and the pictures . . . well, they sometimes speak for themselves. Gerald Ford, runner-up to Jimmy Carter in 1976, is often depicted as a klutz. And sure enough, his picture keeps falling off the wall.

Small-Town Banks:

Where you can cash a check, get a loan, and learn little-known facts about obscure politicians.

A big, hand-painted wooden sign 25 miles south of Quinter reads PACIFIC OCEAN, 1,265 MILES, ATLANTIC OCEAN, 1,342. But go back a few years—65 million or so—and Kansas had the best oceanfront view in North America. Of course, back then there were no realtors to recognize its value.

During the late Cretaceous Period (87 to 65 million years ago), Kansas teemed not with land sharks but with 20-foot sea sharks that could crunch clamshells like sunflower seeds. They swam in the ocean next to squid, oysters, plesiosaurs, pterandodons, and 25-foot mosasaurs with teeth 4 inches long.

All that remain now are wide expanses of chalk canyons, but for paleontologists and other fossil hunters, these canyons provide some of the best Cretaceous marine fossils in the world. Noteworthy finds include an 85-million-year-old mosasaur skull (now in actor Charlie Sheen's collection) and the most photographed fossil in the world: a 14-foot Xiphactinus that swallowed a 6-foot Gillicus. It resides in the Sternberg Museum of Natural History in Hays.

Most major natural history museums own specimens from the area, a 600-mile swath of western Kansas known as the Smoky Hills Chalk Formation. Even though it has been a hotbed for collectors for more than 135 years (professors from Yale came to dig as early as 1870 and claimed nearly 2,000 mosasaurs for the university's prestigious Peabody Museum), there are still thousands of feet of marine sediment left to explore.

Smoky Hills Chalk Formation:

The result of a vast marine sea that covered much of western Kansas millions of years ago.

If you're going to open an indoor water park in a town with a famous space museum, you're pretty much limited in your choice of themes. You could go with the space theme. Or there's the space theme. Or . . . well, let's just say it was inevitable.

When the Grand Prairie Hotel in Hutchinson opened its 27,000-square-foot indoor water park, designers had little choice but to name it Kansas Splashdown and to make sure that all its attractions were space-related. Not only is the hot tub disguised as a moon crater, but the lazy river meanders around a "moon base," and the dump bucket looks like a Mercury rocket that counts down before blasting off with a torrent of water.

If your child wants to celebrate a birthday at Splashdown, he can choose a lunar party, a rocket party, or a blast-off party. As far as I know, it's the only space water park in the world.

The Kansas Cosmosphere, the famous space museum that swayed the water park's destiny, was started in a poultry barn in 1962. Like the space program it honors, it has come a long way. Today the museum has the world's largest collection of space suits, an SR-71 spy plane, an astronaut

Space:

The inspiration for great museums and water parks, not to mention exploration beyond our planet.

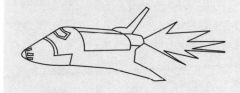

training jet, the actual Apollo 13 command module, and a full-scale space shuttle replica. Second only to Washington, D.C.'s National Air and Space Museum in the number of space artifacts, the Cosmosphere also offers space camps for kids of all ages, leases space artifacts to museums all over the world, and even consults with Hollywood stars filming space movies.

you know you're in
kansas when...
...big rocks are taken for granted

We've got lots of rocks in Kansas, rocks that if they were located anywhere else would have millions of tourists streaming by them. Rock City, for example, near Minneapolis, has 200 house-size rocks in the space of two football fields. It's the only place in the world with so many monster concretions. And, yes, this geological wonder has been designated a National Landmark.

But don't expect a concession stand. In fact, just finding the place is an achievement of note. The signs leading there are minuscule, the roads are dirt, and you start to wonder what fool notion ever propelled you into wanting to see these huge sandstone concretions in the first place.

Until you arrive. And then you're dumbstruck. How did these huge rocks get here? And what the heck are you supposed to do with them? You can't exactly skip them. Or build houses out of them. About all you can do is name them after what they most resemble and crawl on top . . . if you can make it up there.

But first you have to deposit your $3.00 entry fee in the rusted contribution box and sign your name in the registry, a 39-cent notebook like the kind you used in second grade. Once you've done that, you're free to wander around Turtle Rock, Kissing Lips, the Twin Sisters, and 197 other monster rocks.

The Stone Age:

Still in existence in Kansas.

There are also five acres of mushroom-shaped rocks near Ellsworth and a big rock in McLouth, smack dab in the middle of Granite Street, between Cynthia and Lucy. The latter specimen has been paved around more than a few times, but it's still big enough to cause undercarriage damage if you happen to forget it's there. Back in the mid-1970s, the local street department decided to remove the famous rock, but when they tried to excavate, they discovered it was so big that the job would bankrupt city coffers.

In the 1970s Kansas had some rather strange liquor laws (nobody could drink without a membership). Vern Miller, our hyperactive attorney general, attempted to enforce them even on airplanes flying over the state. He justified his ruling by saying, "Kansas goes all the way up, and Kansas goes all the way down."

The airlines laughed at him, of course, and far as I know, nobody ever put down his gin-and-tonic when flying across the Kansas border. But Vern Miller did have a point. We Kansans have a thing about our skies. We watch them. We take the time to look at our stars. Our clouds. We know which ones are capable of turning against us.

And our sunsets, well, they can make a person go weak in the knees. We've got colors that Crayola hasn't even thought up yet. And talk about wide-screen. While we don't throw nightly sunset celebrations like they do in Key West and Clearwater Beach, and we don't applaud or have sword-swallowers, we do tend to pause for a moment and notice that another day is going out in a fit of glory. We watch our sunsets in silence, usually alone or with a friend or a family member or two. But just because we don't have tightrope walkers and Uncle Sam look-alikes giving away $22 bills doesn't mean that we don't appreciate what we've got here. We just prefer to give our skies the reverence they deserve.

Sunset:

1. The daily disappearance of the sun below the western horizon. 2. A time of day when most Kansans are in awe.

Although Warner Brothers chose to film *Superman Returns* on a farm in Tamworth, Australia, everybody knows it's supposed to be Kansas. After all, Kansas is where adoptive parents Jonathan and Martha Kent raised the young superhero, on a farm near Smallville. The Man of Steel's birth parents, Jor-El and Lara, were from Planet Krypton. When they learned that their planet was doomed to catastrophic destruction, they sent their only son to Earth, where he crashed in a cornfield near the Kents' farm.

For years we knew only that Smallville was somewhere in the heart of America. But in a 1986 comic, the man who was more powerful than a locomotive, faster than a speeding bullet, and able to leap tall buildings in a single bound made the comment, "At heart, I'm just a boy from a small town in Kansas." It was in Kansas that Superman learned the values of courage and valor, hallmarks of his heroic nature.

Like most Kansans, Superman has amazing strength, enjoys X-ray vision, and is highly impervious to physical harm. Unfortunately, the rest of us Kansans can't fly. Except when lifted by powerful twisters, of course.

Superman:

1. Beloved comic book character created in 1938 by DC Comics. 2. A big celebrity from Kansas who moved to Metropolis and went underground as a mild-mannered reporter for the *Daily Planet*.

We're proud of our grass here in Kansas. Some say a cow can gain two and a half pounds per day eating blue stem, switchgrass, Indian grass, or any of the other 400 grasses that make up our Kansas prairies. That's why millions of cattle are sent to the Flint Hills each spring for what many ranchers consider the finest bovine dining in the world.

When pioneers first reached Kansas, the tallgrass was daunting, to say the least—higher in many patches than a man on a horse. They called it the "inland sea." Today, the Tallgrass Prairie National Preserve near Cottonwood Falls is the last great stand of tallgrass prairie left in the United States. It's our only national park dedicated to an ecosystem that once covered 140 million acres from southern Texas all the way to Canada. The other three remaining tallgrass prairies are in Sudan, South America, and Russia.

Before the white man's arrival, the Plains Indians used 100 species of prairie grasses for food and another 200 for medicine. Today there's a mere 2 percent of virgin tallgrass prairie left, most of it in Kansas.

Tallgrass Prairie:

A huge, waving sea of grasses that once covered most of central United States. Some five million acres remain in the Flint Hills of east-central Kansas.

you know you're in
kansas when...
...a wildcat does one-arm pushups at halftime

The Kansas State University mascot started as a live bobcat named Touchdown. He lived in a cage on the campus near Nichols Hall. Students used to parade him around the basketball arena and the football stadium at halftime.

Eventually, Touchdown retired to the Manhattan Zoo, and a high school cheerleader dressed as an orange-and-brown wildcat performed gymnastics at halftime. Needless to say, fans were aghast. Their beloved wildcat looked way too much like a girl and like, well . . . an inferior feline from a competing college.

By 1964 Willie, a madcap wildcat who wears a football jersey and a fierce head, took over the job that includes whipping up crowd enthusiasm and taunting opponents' mascots, most of whom are encumbered in clunky costumes and can't get around as well as Willie in his sleek jersey. Clandestine tryouts are held every year; members of the cheerleading squad, the only students who know Willie's true identity, are sworn to secrecy.

Tigers, Sooners, and Huskers:

College mascots that, as a Kansan, you are required to despise.

you know you're in
kansas when...
...basements are called storm shelters

Thanks to L. Frank Baum, Kansas will always be associated with tornadoes. And there's no dismissing the fact the state sits smack dab in the center of Tornado Alley, an area defined by the American Meteorology Society as the "highest in tornado frequency."

Admittedly, Kansas has racked up a few. There used to be a town called Irving in northeastern Kansas; it was hit by two tornadoes in one day, something weather forecasters claim is a statistical impossibility. In another myth-spreading incident, a twister struck what used to be Codell (in Reno County) on May 20 of 1916, 1917, and 1918. May 20, 1919, I'm happy to report, was a beautiful spring day.

At first the tornado reputation was a bit distressing. But now tornadoes are one of those lemons squeezed into lemonade. Kansans proudly sign up to be tornado spotters. And numerous companies take tourists on weeklong tornado-chasing tours. After all, tornadoes have no peer when it comes to meteorological phenomena.

Hurricanes are closest, but look at the facts: Hurricanes cause flooding; tornadoes cause implosions. Hurricanes are given names of old people (Ivan, Frances, Hugo); tornadoes get labels that sound more appropriate for military hardware (an F-4, for example). With hurricanes, affected residents typically get ample warning and have time to evacuate; most tornadoes, on the other hand, just drop from the sky, pick up livestock, and move them several counties over.

Avid funnel junkies count sightings of different types of tornadoes—such as wedges, stovepipes, and ropes—the way that bird watchers mark off marbled murrelets or loggerhead shrikes.

Tornado:

Aka twister, funnel, Dorothy nemesis. In Kansas, a tornado warning siren is your signal to go out in the front yard and look for a funnel.

When you're actually *in* Kansas, people don't ask about Toto. Mainly because they've heard the same inquiry dozens, if not hundreds, of times themselves. It's when you're outside Kansas and you tell someone that you're *from* there that the question comes up. The person who asks it always gets a big chuckle, thinking that he or she is extremely clever and original.

We usually just chuckle right back and say something like, "I left him with Auntie Em." What we really want to say is, "I'll get you, my pretty, and your little dog joke, too."

As ubiquitous as the Toto joke is, you'd think *The Wizard of Oz* was number one on the American Film Institute's list of 100 Greatest American Movies of All Time instead of number six. I guess we should just be thankful that when MGM bought the movie rights, the studio changed Toto to a dog. In the 1902 musical version, Dorothy's companion was a cow (or rather, a human playing a cow) named Imogene. Can you imagine being asked over and over again, "Where's Imogene?" Or Dorothy saying, "Run, Imogene, run"?

Toto:

1. A small dog who accompanies Dorothy on her journey to Oz. 2. An invisible entity that travels with anyone from Kansas.

you know you're in
kansas when...
...tree stumps are popular tourist draws

Council Grove has not one, not two, but three celebrated tree stumps. The town's name, in fact, came from one of the stumps back when it was still a 70-foot-tall, 16-foot-wide tree. Called Council Oak, it was the official council site for the Osage Indians. When government officials decided to seek permission for settlers to pass safely through Osage land, they scheduled a pow-wow under the tree. That was in August 1825. In return for $800, the big cheese of the Osage signed a treaty agreeing not to disturb stagecoaches, wagon trains, and assorted migrants heading down the Santa Fe Trail. Unfortunately, the tree was knocked down by wind in 1958, but the stump is still there, attracting visitors.

Tourists can also see the remains of Post Office Oak, which became nothing but a stump in 1990, when the 300-year-old bur oak bit the dust. In its heyday, it served as the official post office for travelers on the Santa Fe Trail. Between 1825 and 1847, travelers going one way left mail in a hole at the bottom of the tree for travelers going the other way. Letters must have been addressed something like this: "George Custer, Council Grove Oak."

Which brings up the last famous stump in Council Grove. It's called Custer Elm, and it, too, is no longer a whole tree. It's named for General George Custer, who, before his

Tree Stumps:

Cause for celebration in Council Grove. There's even a map for a walking tour, available at the local convention and visitors bureau.

ill-fated rendezvous at Little Bighorn, owned the land it sits on.

Although these stumps are nothing but shadows of their former selves, they are being treated to a fine retirement under fancy canvases in this historic city on the old Santa Fe Trail.

you know you're in
kansas when...
...people from Japan call to order tumbleweeds

Prairie Tumbleweed Farm in Garden City is living proof that you can sell absolutely anything over the Internet.

Linda Katz was just kidding when she asked her son to create a family Web site offering tumbleweeds for sale. Calling the business Prairie Tumbleweed Farm, she listed big tumbleweeds at $35, midsize ones at $25, and economy-size ones at $20. Was Linda ever surprised that after only two months on the Web, the site had received more than 2,000 hits. Soon she had a $1,000 order for the children's TV show *Barney & Friends*.

Never mind that Katz didn't have a farm at all (rather, she lived in a subdivision) and had never even so much as touched a tumbleweed. She quickly recruited her five nieces and nephews to gather tumbleweeds—not a difficult task in western Kansas, where they're known to clog drainage ditches, pile up along fences, and occasionally cause traffic disturbances.

Tumbleweed:

1. A densely branched plant that breaks off from its roots and is rolled about by the wind. 2. A Kansas commodity.

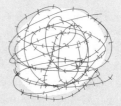

Tumbleweeds from Katz's "farm" are boxed and shipped to addresses all over the world. Customers include TV and movie producers, home decorators, NASA (engineers used them to develop the Tumbleweed Rover for exploring Mars), and some nutty folks who prefer the Russian thistle bushes over Christmas trees. Tumbleweeds are so popular in Japan that Katz now has a Japanese-language version of her Web site.

you know you're in
kansas when...
...the main crop hails from Iraq

Kansas, often referred to as the Breadbasket of the World, produces more wheat than any other state: 374 million bushels every year, more than one-fifth of all wheat grown in the United States. But interestingly enough, the crop that grows on nine million Kansas acres is not native to the Wheat State; it originated in Iraq, Iran, and Syria, where it was domesticated 10,000 years ago by nomadic hunters and gatherers.

Because the once-wild wheat these nomads cultivated was highly nutritious and didn't need preservation, it allowed them to settle down, establish villages, and begin trading for their needs. Eventually wheat became the world's major food staple, spreading from what was known as the Fertile Crescent to Egypt, Central Asia, and Europe.

Columbus introduced wheat to the New World on his second voyage; the first crop was harvested as early as 1494. Kansas got its wheat from Russian immigrants, who brought it in 1874. Although it has been modified and improved, the Turkey Red variety that Russians planted in Kansas is the ancestor of all U.S. Hard Red Winter wheat.

Ironically, more than half of the Kansas wheat crop is exported back to the very area that first domesticated the now-ubiquitous grain. The U.S. government buys a huge percentage of Kansas wheat for overseas food aid, sending some five million tons to areas suffering from war, floods, drought, and other calamities.

Turkey Red:

The Russian wheat variety that established Kansas's reputation for being the breadbasket of the world.

Valeda III, the life-size transparent talking woman of the Kansas Learning Center for Health in Halstead, has taught thousands of Kansas kids how their veins and arteries operate. She's shown them her own nerves, heart, and lymphatic system, all of which light up when she mentions them in a 15-minute presentation on how the body works.

Mounted on a rotating pedestal, Valeda is the featured attraction of the health center, which was started years ago by the Hertzler Foundation—named for Arthur Hertzler, a Kansas doc who traveled the state in a horse and buggy.

Valeda, of course, didn't travel in the buggy. She wasn't even made until 1965, when a woman in Cologne, Germany, allowed a transparent rubber compound to be slopped on her body and left until it dried. The hardened material was peeled off and used as a mold for Valeda's skin.

Valeda who is 5 feet, 7 inches tall and would weigh 145 pounds if she weren't made out of plastic, has several sisters around the country, but according to the folks at the Halstead Center, she's the only

Valeda III:

A life-size transparent anatomical mannequin with light-up organs, 6¼ miles of red- and blue-coated wires, and an instructional voice track recorded in 1965.

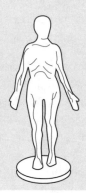

one who talks. One of her predecessors in Chicago was almost named "Cassie, the Lassie with the Glassy Chassis." Luckily for Valeda III, whose moniker came from her Chicago counterpart, that wasn't the final choice.

you know you're in
kansas when...
... a van Gogh painting is the tallest thing in town

Anything that's eight stories high is bound to stand out on the Kansas prairie. In Goodland, within gandering distance of Interstate 70, is a 24- by 32-foot painting of a vase of sunflowers by Vincent van Gogh.

Okay, so it's a reproduction. Canadian artist Cameron Cross decided to reproduce all seven of the sunflower paintings that van Gogh completed in Arles, France, in 1888 and 1889. Cross calls it the Big Easel Project, and he has chosen seven sites in seven countries that have a connection to either van Gogh or sunflowers. (So far, Cross has sunflower paintings in Altona, Canada; Emerald, Australia; and Goodland. If all goes according to plan, he hopes to make the *Guinness Book of World Records*, something the one-eared painter did not accomplish.)

Far as I know, Vincent never made it to Goodland, so I'm guessing that the city's connection is sunflowers. Two sunflower-processing plants, one of which produces oil for Pringles potato chips, are based in this western Kansas town.

van Gogh:

A famous Dutch painter who inspired a sorta famous Canadian painter to think big.

The 80-foot easel for Cross's reproduction weighs 40,000 pounds and requires 30-foot-deep cement pilings just to make sure it doesn't topple over.

you know you're in
kansas when...
...your town has hot and cold water towers

I have a bone to pick with Hubbard, Iowa, and Garrison, North Dakota. Can't you think of anything more original to paint on your water towers? Putting "hot" and "cold" on side-by-side towers is a cute gag, certainly. That's why we Kansans came up with the idea years and years ago.

Pratt has had "hot" and "cold" water towers since 1956 . . . ever since graffiti artists overcame their fear of heights. City fathers liked the idea so much that they made it official, a move that garnered the small town more than a little bit of national publicity. Canton also has "hot" and "cold" towers. A guy I talked to there wasn't sure enough to want to be quoted, but he thought that they had been around since the 1930s.

Okemah, Oklahoma, joined the trend but had the sense to add a third tower that says "Home of Woody Guthrie." I guess that frees it up from the plagiarism charge.

Vandals in another Kansas town didn't meet with the same approval as their Pratt counterparts. Not long after Pfizer introduced the drug Viagra, graffiti artists in Agra climbed their local water tower to add the letters *V* and *I*. How could you blame them? Looking up every morning to see plain *Agra* on the sky-high tower must have been worse than a mosquito bite begging

to be scratched. City fathers, as I mentioned, were not pleased. So they, too, climbed the tower and painted over the added letters.

In other weird Kansas water tower news, Harper's structure has a tomato-red, 9.5-foot iron fish on top of it, supposedly to determine the wind direction. It has been there since 1886, except for a brief period in 1892 when a cyclone knocked it over.

Water Towers:

The perfect palette for Kansas humorists and graffiti artists.

Heck, with half our population making a living at something that depends so dearly on the whims of Mother Nature, whether it's going to rain or snow or sleet or hail or freeze or [*add your own weather condition here*] is clearly an important topic of conversation. Probably the most important.

Not that talking does anything about it. All we can really do is throw up our hands and accept the stark reality that sometimes Kansas is dustbowl dry, and other times our farm fields are nothing but monsoon-soaked mud. Sometimes temps hover above 100 for days on end. Sometimes it's so windy that clothes hung on an outside line end up 2 miles down the road at the Jones's barn.

But we still like to talk about it. And talk about it some more. And stay up until 10:19 P.M., when our local weather forecasters dispense the good or bad news for the following day. I've heard that the water pressure in Kansas swells at exactly 10:23 each night, when all the farmers click off the news and head to the bathroom for one last flush before retiring for the night.

Weather:

Because of its significance to our economy and well-being, a popular conversation starter.

you know you're in
kansas when...
...five other states tried to steal your state bird

The 121,000 kids of Kansas who voted in the western meadowlark (which barely beat out the bobwhite and cardinal) as the state bird on January 29, 1925, didn't say for sure, but I suspect that their decision was swayed by the fact that the meadowlark's main food source is grasshoppers.

We'll do anything around here to honor anybody or anything that helps us get rid of pesky grasshopper swarms, which have been known to get thick enough to block out the sun. In 1874, during one of the worst plagues on record, grasshoppers ate crops out of the ground, wool off live sheep, and clothing off our own new pioneers' backs. Not exactly a welcoming introduction.

The other feature we like about our state bird is that its song, a beautiful flute-like warble, would easily win *American Idol* if the producers should decide to host an avian series. The western meadowlark's voice is often used on movie sound tracks—even movies set in places where western meadowlarks don't live.

Western Meadowlark:

A robin-size songbird with a yellow breast, black bib, and mottled brown body. Not to be confused with the eastern meadowlark, whose singing voice is far inferior.

I hate to break it to the five copycats that also designated the western meadowlark their state bird—Montana, Nebraska, North Dakota, Oregon, and Wyoming—but we chose it first. Of course, we can't blame you for recognizing genius when you see it.

Even though Kansas is often referred to as the Wheat State, the beef industry rakes in twice as much moolah as wheat. Depending on the year, Kansas ranks either first or second in the country in the number of commercial cattle processed.

Yes, that's even more than that wannabe down south commonly known as Texas. In fact, cattle from the Lone Star State and other places are regularly shipped to Kansas to fatten up on our nutritious, tall-grass prairie before moving on to slaughter. As many as a million "cattle tourists" summer in the Flint Hills, one of only four remaining tallgrass prairies in the world, and the only one in the US of A.

Kansas also has a huge slaughter and meat-packing industry. Holcomb, with a population of only 2,000, employs more than 3,000 people (go figure) at its meat-processing plant, billed as the world's largest. Although we politely call what they do "processing cattle," there's no getting around the fact that beef-packing plants whack and dismember creatures that weigh up to half a ton.

So many immigrants come to work at the Holcomb plant that, at last count, there were 21 different Asian dialects spoken in nearby Garden City.

Where's the Beef?:

A popular advertising slogan that has a simple answer: Kansas.

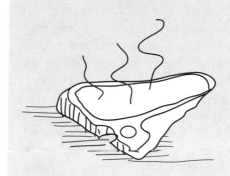

you know you're in
kansas when...

...your hometown is featured daily in more than 1,000 newspapers

Wichita, the largest city in Kansas, shows up every day on the funny pages of more than 1,000 newspapers in 48 countries and in 19 different languages.

You may not notice the Century II Convention Center, the 700 statues Gino Salerno carved out of dead trees, the sailboat that won the America's Cup one year, or other popular Wichita landmarks—but I bet you are familiar with the Wichita street where five-year-old Dennis "the Menace" Mitchell lives with his patient parents, Henry and Alice Mitchell; his dog, Ruff; and his cat, Hot Dog. Henry works at a local aeronautics company (cartoonist Hank Ketchum never said whether it was Boeing, Cessna, or one of the other half-dozen Wichita aircraft companies), and George Wilson, Dennis's grouchy neighbor, is retired from the city post office.

Other notable Wichita sites are a pyramid (located at the Olive W. Garvey Center for the Improvement of Human Functioning), which was used for energy experiments before it became a conference center and restaurant; the Museum of World Trea-

sures, where you can see a real Egyptian mummy and the autograph of every U.S. president; the Pioneer Balloon Company, which produces a million latex balloons every day, including those released on Times Square each New Year's Eve; and the world's first Pizza Hut.

Wichita Attractions:

There's plenty for Dennis "the Menace" to do in Wichita, Kansas's largest city.

you know you're in
kansas when...
... each couple gets their own square mile

According to the 2000 Census, Wallace County in western Kansas has a population of 1,749 and enough square miles (914) that every 1.9 people get their own. Compare that to New York County, which has 67,000 people for every square mile.

Granted, you don't get many Broadway plays or city parks wrapped by Christo in Wallace County, especially now that the sugar beet plant went belly-up, but you do get a free county fair every July and a view of Mount Sunflower, the highest point in Kansas at 4,039 feet. (If you need directions, check with Barney at the only gas station in Weskan.) A plaque on the mountain reads NOTHING HAPPENED HERE IN 1897.

There's also the Rattlesnake Roundup, an event that attracts thousands to Sharon Springs each Mother's Day weekend. You can not only sample rattlesnake meat (I dare you to find a restaurant in Manhattan that lists rattler on its menu), but also watch Fangs and Rattlers, a touring exhibition team, perform such tricks as stuffing 12 live snakes into a sleeping bag with a live man in it. Find the biggest rattler yourself, and you'll take home $100 in prize money and a trophy.

Wide-Open Space:

A synonym for much of Kansas, including Wallace County.

...people think your only claim to fame is a giant ball of string

It's true: Kansas does have the world's largest ball of twine. And folks—as many as 300,000 per year, I've heard—come from across the globe to gawk at the nine-ton monstrosity that's displayed in an open-air gazebo in downtown Cawker City. The guest book indicates that one couple from Salt Lake City drove nine hours out of their way for this once-in-a-lifetime photo op.

It's also true that the Kansas ball has imitators—one in Darwin, Minnesota, and one in Branson, Missouri. Both have the gall to claim victory over their Kansas counterpart, which exhausts every fourth grader who tries to run around it. All I know is that our contender was started in 1953 by farmer Frank Stoeber, who accidentally tripped over a piece of hay bale twine one hot August afternoon. Within four years of that fateful meeting, Stoeber's new hobby stood 8 feet tall and weighed 5,000 pounds.

In a fit of patriotic fervor, Stoeber donated the ball to Cawker City during the state centennial in 1961. His legacy lives on in the annual Twine-a-Thon, held on the third Friday in August. That's when volunteers show up to add more string So na-na-na-na-boo-boo to you wannabes in Minnesota and Missouri—our ball gets bigger by the year.

World's Largest Ball of Twine:

This Cawker City wonder, 12 feet in diameter, is featured in the Chevy Chase movie *Vacation*.

But the real joke is on the folks who think our "king of string" is the only known tourist draw. At the risk of having my citizenship revoked, I will tell you that Kansas also has a mini Grand Canyon and dozens of one-of-a-kind geological wonders. We just choose to keep the good stuff to ourselves.

you know you're in
kansas when...
... a U.S. highway is called the Yellow Brick Road

If you look at a Kansas map published before 2003, when the state legislature introduced House Bill 2135, you might have trouble finding the Yellow Brick Road. That's because it was previously known as U.S. Highway 54. Signs that dot the highway now—at least the 379.6 miles of it that traverse southern Kansas—bear both names.

As far as legislative bills go, 2135, which officially renamed US 54, was a no-brainer—certainly less controversial than the evolution vs. creationism issue that keeps the Kansas government busy and in the national headlines nearly every session.

In the same bill, legislators also renamed the 55.8 miles of Kansas Highway 99 between U.S. Highway 36 and Interstate 70. The bill states that "the secretary of transportation shall place signs along the highway right-of-way at proper intervals to indicate that the highway is 'The Road to Oz.'" I haven't seen her out there with her hammer and nails, but at least she's got permission.

The Yellow Brick Road:

An official highway in Kansas a few miles south of the Road to Oz.

THE YELLOW
BRICK ROAD

index

THE INSIDER'S SOURCE